ENGLISH FOLKLORE

First Edition 1930
A.R. Wright F.S.A

New Edition 2021
Edited by Tarl Warwick

COPYRIGHT AND DISCLAIMER

FOREWORD

This little work is a fine collection of both then-dated and then-contemporary "vulgar" lore in the British Isles- it is simultaneously applauded for academic purposes, and derided as silliness, by the author, in an era marked by the first real interest in folklore collection as a valid institution in the sense comprehended by English academics, post-dating Grimm's collections and other works in other lands by a century.

A great proportion of all of this lore is related to luck, marriage (and courting), or life and death. A large portion has a religious, usually Christian bent, although the pagan origins of many practices- later modified in accordance with spiritual orthodoxy- are often mentioned. The work is quite dense. A few paragraphs had to be shifted simply because they had been broken up in places which did not make sense in the initial volume.

Of especial note is the role of the Great War (World War One) on some superstitions, especially related to ghost lights and tales of the woeful revenants of dead Germans washed ashore in some coastal regions, and their continual apparitional presence.

This edition of "English Folklore" has been carefully edited for format and content. Care has been taken to retain all original intent and meaning.

ENGLISH FOLKLORE

INTRODUCTION

In 1725 Henry Bourne dedicated to those "Incouragers of Learning and Rewarders of Merit," the Mayor and Corporation of the town and county of Newcastle-upon-Tyne, where he was curate of All Saints' Church, a little book with the title *Antiquitates Vulgares*, or "The Antiquities of the Common People. Giving An Account of several of their Opinions and Ceremonies. With Proper Reflections upon each of them; shewing which may be retained and which ought to be laid aside." The mixture of affable condescension to the "common people," and of humble apology to their "betters" for a display of interest in what vulgar folk did and thought, makes the book delightful reading nowadays. The preface says: "I would not be thought a Reviver of old Rites and Ceremonies to the Burdening of the People, nor an Abolisher of innocent Customs, which are their Pleasures and Recreations: I aim at nothing, but a Regulation of those which are in Being among them, which they themselves are far from thinking burdensome, and abolishing such only as are sinful and wicked."

Customs which Bourne regarded with disfavor still flourish lustily, while the religious "observation" of Saturday afternoon and other practices which he applauded have long ago faded into oblivion, but interest in the matters of which he wrote with deprecation has continuously grown. This first book on English folklore was expanded by others into the well-known volumes of what is generally named, after an editor of half a century later. Brand's "Popular Antiquities" In The *Athenaeum* of August 22, 1846, W. J. Thoms, for long secretary of the Camden Society and editor of Notes and Queries, proposed, under a pseudonym, the collection of "what we in England designate as Popular Antiquities, or Popular Literature... which would be most aptly described by a good Saxon compound Folk-Lore, the Lore of the People." The word then coined, and since deprived of its hyphen, has been adopted for the science in almost all civilized languages except the German, which uses the somewhat wider Volkskunde (admitting, however, the adjectival Folklorist or Volklorist).

It was not at first understood that the curious items, unconsidered "trifles, light as air," which fill the pages of Bourne and Brand and other early collections at home and abroad, were yet to the student...

"confirmations strong
As proofs of holy writ,"

...could tell us about their background of the folk mind and unwritten folk history, and could throw light on the beginnings of almost all other sciences. As this has come to be perceived, folklore has gained steadily in influence and scope since the early days when Andrew Lang summarized, in his Adventures Among Books, the lesson "of what we call folklore... which to many seems trivial, to many seems dull. It may become the most attractive and serious of the sciences." "The topic of folklore and the development of customs and myths is not generally attractive, to be sure. Only a few people seem interested in that spectacle, so full of surprises- the development of all human institutions, from fairy tales to democracy. In beholding it we learn how we owe all things, humanly speaking, to the people and to genius. The natural people, the folk, has supplied us, in its unconscious way, with the stuff of all our poetry, law, ritual: and genius has selected from the mass, has turned customs into codes, nursery tales into romance, myth into science, ballad into epic, magic mummery into gorgeous ritual... The student of this lore can look back and see the long trodden way behind him, the winding tracks through marsh and forest and over burning sands. He sees the caves, the camps, the villages, the towns where the race has tarried, for shorter times or longer, strange places many of them, and strangely haunted, desolate dwellings and inhospitable. But the scarce visible tracks converge at last on the beaten ways, the ways to that city whither mankind is wandering."

Folklore, then, has evolved from a record of old women's chatter and rustic festivals into a science dealing with the whole of folk thought and practice. It might be defined as the science which studies the expression, in popular beliefs, institutions, practices, oral literature, and arts and pastimes, of the mental and spiritual life of the folk, the people in general, in every stage of barbarism and culture. It is at the base of all other sciences, and appears in all of them at their early stages, and often survives to a late one; thus, astronomy has evolved out of astrology, and chemistry out of alchemy. Scientific medicine is the child of medical folklore, and has retained in its pharmacopoeia until quite recent years such folk medicines as mummy-powder and pulverized toad, and still uses at the head of its prescriptions a sign which is probably in reality the astrological sign for Jupiter, as a written charm or an invocation of the protecting god.

Folklore seeks to decipher the unwritten history of the folk and the effect on it of heredity and surroundings, and to determine the origins of modern social institutions, customs, and beliefs. It distinguishes the phases of character and motives of conduct which influence national life, and is hence a study of special importance and utility in the British Empire, the home of innumerable races the governing springs of whose conduct are vastly different from our own, and can only be ascertained by the sympathetic study of their folklore. It was the belief that sepoys were compelled to use for their cartridges grease from the cow sacred to Hindus that brought about the Indian Mutiny. The official, the missionary, the doctor, the judge, and the trader ought, therefore, all to be equipped with knowledge of the customs and beliefs of the people to whom they are sent. This applies also to those of us left at home. Folklore is the key to understanding and sympathy with the folk around us. Up to the time of the

Renaissance the culture of all classes was much the same, and King Cophetua's beggar maid had little to learn on her introduction to court circles except to wear richer clothes and eat strange meats. All classes enjoyed together the mumming play and the wandering minstrel's songs and tales. Now education and outside habit have divided us into "classes" and "masses," though the man about town who turns his chair round three times to change his luck at cards is still own brother under the skin to the coster who bows to the new moon or spits on his first money of the day for luck, and the fisherman who spits on his bait or in the mouth of the first fish caught; the Society woman who visits the Bond Street clairvoyant, or palmist, or crystal-gazer has the same longing' to divine the future as her East End sister for whom the greasy cards are turned over in the back street, or the leaves in the teacup are read by an old woman. The educated man should seek to appreciate the immemorial reasons at the back of the mind and actions of the unlettered, and should humble himself by examining his own irrational deeds- crack-stepping as he walks the pavement, avoiding ladders and thirteen at table, and so on. Then, too, folklore is essential to the full enjoyment of our literature. The plays of Shakespeare are full of it, and only folklore can explain such passages as that in the soliloquy of King Henry VI (Third Part, Act II., sc. v.):

> "O God! methinks it were a happy life
> To be no better than a homely swain;
> To sit upon a hill, as I do now.
> To carve out dials quaintly, point by point."

This is made clear by Mr. Lovett's discovery of the remarkable sundials still cut in the turf by the shepherds of the South Downs, and King Henry evidently refers to these turf dials and not to pocket dials of wood. Similarly, the Folk-Lore of the Old Testament has been written at length by Sir James Frazer, and the science has decisive evidence to give as regards the antiquity of the matter of the Hebrew Scriptures.

ENGLISH FOLKLORE

Lastly, "the proper study of mankind is man," and folklore is such a study in which every man and every woman can play a part: the housewife can gather local cures, superstitions, ideas of luck and ill-luck, tales, sayings, and other items from villagers and townsfolk, whichever she may meet, and from servants and charwomen; the tourist, in fair weather and foul, from the road-mender, the shepherd, the innkeeper, the farmer, and the country railway porter; the book-lover and the invalid from the books they read and from their attendants and visitors. In short, all can at least collect the material which is the very life-blood of the subject, even if they leave its ultimate interpretation to the scholar in his room, far withdrawn from the noise of streets and farms. But need not labor further the obvious utilities and advantages of the study, and the innumerable points it which it seeks aid from, and gives help to, other studies. The science is yet young, its surprising results are not always finally defined, and its literature is voluminous. A competent library of folklore in general must include some thousands of voiles and pamphlets in many languages, and- to name only three examples of recent works in different departments of the whole- the last edition of Sir James Frazer's *Golden Bough* comprises twelve volumes and 4,513 pages, Professor Westermarck's *History of Human Marriage* three volumes and 1,795 pages, and his *Ritual and Belief in Morocco* two volumes and 1,286 pages. It is, therefore, not easy to give a connected and intelligible idea of the whole field of the science in a short space.

> "Can this cockpit hold
> The vasty fields of France?"

Even a review of British folklore alone would lead us far afield, for there is within the boundaries of these isles a patchwork of races with distinctive features in their folklores only to be explained by comparison with those of races abroad. For instance, in the Channel Islands, which were of much consequence in prehistoric times, we have in Guernsey the procession of the

Chevauchee de St. Michel, which needs comparison with perambulatory ceremonials in Brittany. In our examination of the Danelagh of East England we must refer to Denmark as well as Germany, and for the Orkneys and elsewhere to Scandinavia. These British areas all differ greatly from each other in their folklore, but the differences are no less between Man and the Midlands, Galway and the Scilly Islands, or Wessex and the Highlands. Any investigation of British folklore as a whole must accordingly deal of necessity with the comparisons which are truly malodorous when compressed into small bulk.

The present purpose is much less ambitious. It is only to draw attention to the richness, perhaps by many readers hardly suspected, of the living folklore of England. It is often difficult to say when a practice or belief is quite dead and gone, many apparently destroyed by the late war having reappeared after an interval, and others being found still lingering in forgotten corners. It will be remembered that the traditional cockfighting at Easter, supposed to have been suppressed long ago, was found, in 1927, to have been still taking place for many years in the greatest secrecy in the Lake District. Our limitation will therefore be to what has been active during the last generation, but in most cases also to what has been noted after the war. This restriction will remove from our present ken such huge subjects as King Arthur and his knights, the legend of the Holy grail, medieval romance cycles, Anglo-Saxon and Celtic magic and leechcraft, etc., which fully deserve treatment in separate volumes.

The following chapters, in consequence, contain no more than samples, taken to some extent at random so as not to favor preconceived notions, of certain classes of current English folkore. To larger works will be left questions of origins and diffusion, of animism and preanimism, of mother-right and father-right, of vegetation souls and separable external souls (sent out in sleep, or kept by the giant or ogre or magician of folktale in a safe place), and such matters of theory and deduction. The present book will have achieved all its aims if some readers are induced to aid in the great enterprise of recording what remains of the heritage of our folk from the past and what is being created by them for the future.

ENGLISH FOLKLORE

BIRTH, COURTSHIP, MARRIAGE, AND DEATH

Mr. Stanley Baldwin said in 1926: "On the day that I was born, our cook, who was a Bewdley woman, wrapped me in a blanket, and to insure I should rise in life she did the proper thing- she carried me up some stairs. But she wanted my life to be a considerable one, so she tramped up to the top of the house, and when she got there she put a chair on the middle of one of the attic rooms, got on it with me in her arms, and then held me up." In these words the Prime Minister sets out the traditional theory and practice of mothers and nurses when the baby leaves its mother's room for the first time. But the folklore of birth begins at an even earlier stage. One of the customs which has excited most surprise and interest in students is that of the couvade ("hatching"), or "man-childbed," which is found to exist among certain South American Indians and other peoples, with whom, after a birth, the mother immediately goes about her usual duties, while the father rests in bed, is well nourished, and receives congratulatory visits from his friends. There are traces of this idea of the vicarious sufferings of the husband in England, where in London, Cheshire, Oxfordshire, and elsewhere it is believed that in some cases the wife's ailments are borne by the husband, who endures neuralgia and "morning sickness" in place of the expectant mother. It is thought that "a good nut year is a good baby year."

The day of birth is important as an augury of the baby's future life. Most people are familiar with some variant or other of the North Country Hues:

"Monday's child is fair of face,
Tuesday's child is full of grace,
Wednesday's child is full of woe.
And Thursday's child has far to go.
Friday's child is loving and giving.
And Saturday's child has to work for a living.

ENGLISH FOLKLORE

But the bairn that is born on the Sabbath day
Is bonny and lucky and wise and gay."

A Cornish version is:

"Sunday's child is full of grace.
Monday's child is full in the face.
Tuesday's child is solemn and sad.
Wednesday's child is merry and glad.
Thursday's child is inclined to thieving.
Friday's child is free in giving.
Saturday's child works hard for his living."

All forms seem to agree on the good luck of the Sunday child.

The time as well as the day of birth is important, as it is generally believed that children born early in the morning have the best chance of long life; the later the birth hour, the shorter the life. In East Anglia, at least, it is thought that those born in the "chime hours" (viz., 12, 4, 8, and 12, or 3, 6, 9, and 12) are specially gifted, as they will be able to see ghosts and spirits. Children are still at times said to come from "the gooseberry bushes," in which ingenious persons have, quite unnecessarily it seems to me, seen a proof of "totemism," by which we claimed descent from the bush.

If the baby is born with a caul (membrane) covering the head, it is "extra lucky" and will not be drowned or hanged, and the caul is generally carefully preserved. In some parts it is regarded as what the folklorist terms a life-index, "overgiving" (weeping) when its owner is ill and withering away at death. There are many signs of the future about the baby. If it has blue vein in its nose, it is born to be drowned. "Mole on the neck, trouble by the peck." According to a Suffolk belief, the first person to kiss the baby "tempers" it, and so you must ask leave of the mother.

ENGLISH FOLKLORE

The folklore of the nursery is very extensive. The Twenty-Eighth Report of the Devonshire Association (1927) tells us that "a large skim-milk cheese is prepared, of which the doctor is to eat the first slice, as soon as the infant is born." In the North a cake is prepared as well as cheese provided, and all relations must eat of it. A piece of the cake and cheese are reserved, to be given (sometimes with the addition of a silver coin to the parcel) by the nurse to the first child or person of opposite sex to the baby met on the way to the christening. Gifts must be brought for the baby by the female relatives and neighbors who call to inspect it and congratulate the mother. In Devon this visit is called the "How d'ye doing" (and by the men "Magpie Fair"), and in Somerset "Shaking out the feathers."

There are many taboos or things prohibited. The baby's hair and nails must not be cut during the first twelve months, but the nails may be bitten short.

> "Cut not its nails until a year
> Has gone; then, mother, have no fear."

If the first nail-parings are buried under an ash tree, this will make the child a "top-singer." During the first year, also, the baby should not see itself in a mirror, but some say that this applies only to the baby being shown itself in the glass. The right hand should not be washed, but only wiped with a damp cloth, "so that he may gather riches." The baby must not be called by the name chosen before it has been baptized, and in London and many parts of the country there is a very strong objection to its being weighed, which seems analogous to the Israelitish objection to the counting of the people (2 Sam. xxiv. 10), but, if an explanation is given, it is generally that any baby put in the scales will die within the year. Curious "Christian" names of babies in the West Country are often due to "pricking the Bible"- taking the first name on a page chosen by inserting a pin between the leaves.

ENGLISH FOLKLORE

The first outdoor trip of the child and mother must be to church for the christening, and before that they would be very unwelcome in any house. When the child is brought for baptism, an open grave in the churchyard forecasts its death within the year, and the north door of the church ought to be left open for the escape of the Devil when driven out by baptism. If the baby does not cry when sprinkled, it is "too good to live," and will probably be reminded of its duty by a sly pinch. If two babies are baptized at the same time, the last taken by the minister will not thrive, and if a boy and a girl appear together at the font, the boy must be christened first, or through life he will be smooth-faced and the girl will have his beard.

There is a sort of faint reminiscence of the ancient "foundation sacrifice" about the notion that the first child baptized in a new font is sure to die. The Huddersfield Examiner (26/11/1910) writes: "At Dalton a new church was built. A blacksmith there had seven daughters, and then a son was born. A few days before the consecration of the new church he came to the vicar, begging him to baptize his boy in the temporary church font. 'Why, Joseph, if you only wait till Thursday the child can be baptized in the new font at the opening of the new church.' Thank you, sir,' said the blacksmith with a wriggle, 'but, you see, it's a lad, and we should be sorry if he were to dee; na, if 't had a bin a lass, why, then, you were welcome, for 'twouldn't 'a' mattered, not a ha'penny. Lasses be ower many, an' lads ower few wi' us.'"

After the christening the child may be taken a-visiting, and at each house should receive some gift- from old-fashioned people an egg, salt, and white bread or cake or a coin, the symbolism of which is obvious. In some neighborhoods the gift is salt or sugar, some tea, and a silver coin. Sometimes the gift is pinned in the baby's clothes till he gets home. According to a Leicestershire belief, there will soon be a new baby in the first family visited by the mother of a first-born, and each friend visited puts a florin in the baby's hand and crosses it for luck, the money not being changed and being spent on the baby's clothing. Each who sees it should hold it for a moment for luck.

We will not follow the nurse further, as she gives the baby "cinder tea" (made by quenching embers in water) for flatulence and colic, or washes it for the first time in water heated by a hot poker or by dropping in hot cinders. Nor will we rock the empty cradle, which would be expected to result in the speedy coming of a fresh occupant. Of the growing child we only mention the consignment of a cast milk-tooth to the fire with the saying, "Good tooth- bad tooth- God send me another good tooth," and remark that the folk say that no bastard can span his own wrist.

Of the lover we say little, as the outlander from another village has no longer to "pay his footing" or to meet strong resentment from his sweetheart's fellow-villagers, and many courting customs have either dropped out of use or have lost their meaning. The exchange of locks of hair no longer implies a voluntary placing of each in the other's power, by the giving of that which would enable evil magic to be worked. Love-charms and divination and marriage omens are dealt with in later chapters. A few taboos still survive. The future should not be anticipated, and therefore an engaged couple should not be photographed together (London) nor be godparents together (a memory of the pre-Reformation prohibition of marriage between godparents), the wedding ring and dress may only be fitted but not worn before the ceremony- some say that the ring ought not even to be tried on beforehand, and that the bride must on no account make her own dress, nor may the lovers meet on the wedding day before they reach the church. When a young German was accidentally killed in 1913 by riding with his motorcycle over the cliff between Brighton and Rottingdean, the local opinion was that this was due to his having seen his Brighton fiancee in her wedding dress.

When we turn to the marriage itself, we find more taboos, some of them very familiar, such as: "If you marry in Lent, you'll live to repent," a memory of Catholic times; "Marry in May and you'll rue the day," May having been an unlucky time for the purpose ever since the days of Ovid, when it was the month of the Roman funeral rites of the Lemuralia. Even in 1928 there was a rush of weddings in the last days of April. The occasional Society marriages in May, in which unlucky green and peacocks' feathers are also flaunted, are an obvious "stunt," like the "Thirteen Club," advertising the existence of "superstition" by professing to defy it.

Easter Sunday, it may be noted here, has for a couple of centuries or so been thought a lucky wedding day by sailor men, and, on account of the holiday, Easter has been favored also by costers and others. Hence Easter Day is now often called "Splice Sunday." Preference is given, not only to particular seasons of the year, but also to particular weekdays as the luckiest, Wednesday being the favorite, as in the rhyme still repeated:

> "Monday for health,
> Tuesday for wealth,
> Wednesday best day of all,
> Thursday for crosses,
> Friday for losses,
> Saturday no luck at all."

The slight prejudice, for it is now no more, against a marriage in which the bride changes her surname but not its initial letter- "Change the name and not the letter, change for the worse and not for the better" has too long a history behind it for discussion now; it was sufficient in a London election in 1922 to injure among the women electors the chances of one of the candidates who had just married someone of the same initial letter. Other taboos, active in one place or another, are that it is unlucky for the bride to hear her banns proclaimed or to see her reflection in the looking-glass when fully dressed for the church, and for the dress to be seen by candlelight. The bride should put her right foot first over the threshold when leaving home for the church, and, in very familiar phrase, she should wear:

> "Something old, something new,
> Something borrowed, something blue."

According to the practice of one county, the old "something" is always the shoes. There are a few special local customs followed on the way to church- e.g., at Rolleston (Notts) the bride may walk through the divided lower part of the trunk of a certain tree, which has somewhat a horseshoe shape, to bring luck. The bride is lucky in her choice if the weather on her wedding day is sunny- "Happy the bride the sun shines on"- and if the clock chimes just before she enters church. To avoid the unhappiness consequent on the clock striking while she is in church, a country bride will wait outside for the chimes to sound. While she is at church the door of her home must not be shut. In one county at least it is very unlucky for a married man or woman to make part of a bridal party, but in a neighboring county it is lucky. A whole treatise would be needed to deal with the folklore of the existing marriage ceremony, which embodies many ancient ideas and is drawn from many sources. Even the bride's dress derives its veil from the Anglo-Saxons and its orange blossoms (replacing the earlier rosemary) from the Saracens.

After the wedding, in North Northumberland there still survives the custom of "jumping the petting stone," a name not yet clearly explained. Only in Holy Island is there an actual fixed stone, but elsewhere two upright stones are placed temporarily, with a stone across their tops, or a wooden bench put across the churchyard gate, and the newly married pair are required to leap the obstruction for luck and to give largesse to those who assist them. The old custom of stopping the way of the pair with a rope until money is paid is now practiced in some villages in Yorkshire. The rice showered before the war in ancient symbolism has now been almost everywhere replaced by the abominable and meaningless "confetti" which disfigure the roadways for so long after a wedding. Probably the change was greatly accelerated during the war by the prosecution, for wasting food, of those who still used rice.

The most interesting and yet puzzling rite of all is the throwing after the newly married of a pair of old shoes, which is universal among English people, but rare among others. It persists so strongly that shoes are even tied to honeymoon aeroplanes. Shoes seem to have been thrown at times of starting other risky undertakings, and may have been intended as a magical means of imparting vital strength, though it is true that in many different countries a pair of shoes is given by the bridegroom to the bride or her relations.

In 1920 an old custom was revived at Irnham in South Lincolnshire, when the bridesmaids carried wooden spoons, which they threw over their heads to the bridegroom as they left the church. When the bride nears her home, in a few districts of Yorkshire, a plate, usually with a cake on it, is thrown over her carriage or herself, and bad is the omen if the plate is not broken, or at least chipped; a slipper may be thrown instead. The bride may still be lifted over the threshold as formerly, and may take a pebble with her into her new home.

Many other rites follow the wedding. Had our subject been history and not merely living practice, much space would have been necessary to treat of the bride cake and wedding gifts. Not long ago a neighbor of mine in London poured boiling water over her doorstep after a son's wedding, "to warm the threshold for the next wedding." A pin out of the bride's veil will secure the speedy marriage of her attendant (or, in some places, prevent it), and bride cake passed through the wedding ring will bring dreams of future wedlock, if placed under the pillow, though some think it unlucky ever to remove the ring. The ring itself can rub away a sty upon the eyelid, and perhaps has shared its virtue with the ring-finger, which is still held to have special healing powers.

The present-day custom at Dunmow in Essex of awarding a flitch of bacon to any married couple who swear that neither of them has ever repented within a twelve-month and a day was formally instituted as a local festival in 1855, subsequent to a claim rejected by the lord of the manor in 1851 on account of long dormancy of the ancient custom. It receives more notice from newspapers than any other local practice, and its revival, or, more properly, its institution under the old name, is a result of Harrison Ainsworth's novel *The Flitch of Bacon*. Very little is recorded of the actual custom of the priory of Little Dunmow and its successor, the manor, but light is thrown upon it by a similar obsolete jocular tenure imposed by John of Gaunt on Whichnor Manor in Staffordshire.

Another post-marriage custom still in existence- wife selling- is referred to in Chapter III., and is a folk method of obtaining divorce, originating days when this was banned by the Church. Death is threatened in advance by innumerable omens, of which a few are mentioned in Chapter VII. While the passing bell probably nowhere tolls to ask prayers for the dying, doors and windows are opened for the escape of the soul at death, and mirrors covered. Death is still expected, especially near the coast, to take place at ebb tide, the soul "going out with the tide," and departure is rendered hard by pigeon or game feathers in the pillow or bed, or by the bed being crosswise to the ceiling beams or flooring boards. Friends and neighbors and strangers flock to see the corpse, and commonly touch it, preferably on the hand, it is now said, to avoid bad dreams or to show that there is no grudge, but in earlier times to guard against haunting. Until at any rate a few years ago, near Sunderland the room in which the corpse was laid was draped all round with sheets and the door fanlight also covered. To keep the body unburied over Sunday is expected to provoke another death within three weeks, but the all-night light and the "watching" of the corpse seem to have ceased. The weather on the funeral day is held to presage the fate of the deceased, for "Blessed is the corpse that the rain rains on."

Aubrey in the seventeenth century described as known in Herefordshire a custom under which bread, a bowl of beer, and sixpence were handed over the corpse to a "sin-eater," who ate and drank and then took upon himself the sins of the deceased, and freed him from "walking." Aubrey adds that the custom was known in Wales, which has been vehemently denied. In 1924 a nurse in North Herefordshire pressed the mother of a dead child to lay a piece of bread on its breast, on the ground that this was customary, and this seems a faint reminiscence of sin-eating. The plate of salt often placed upon a corpse has, of course, another explanation. The clothes of the dead are always believed to decay quickly. As a Northumbrian woman said of house linen which was bequeathed to her and rotted, "they fretted" for their old owner. At Heywood in Lancashire, a short time after the disappearance of an oatcake and crumpet seller, the clothes he left behind him began to rot away, and convinced his family that he was dead. This came out when he turned up after five years and was fined for desertion.

The old pomp and circumstance of the funeral among poor people has been greatly reduced since the war. Only occasionally is there to be seen, except in the East End of London and remote parishes, of late years the nodding black ostrich plumes upon the hearse, once so universal, and there is certainly less eating and (especially) drinking, but the wreaths have, if anything, increased in number. In a woman coster's funeral at Mitcham in October, 1924, over one hundred wreaths, some very elaborate, were piled into the grave above the coffin and were trampled in by two costers, while another took the shovel to fill in the grave himself, and, when remonstrated with by the gravedigger, said that he did it out of respect for the dead. In 1927, according to old custom, more than one hundred men of Tiverton took short turns as voluntary bearers in a funeral where the coffin was carried over three miles and up a hill of 500 feet to a parish church. There are still occasional echoes of the very ancient custom of providing food and other necessaries for the dead. Lights are now and then to be seen upon graves; in one case, at Nantwich in 1926, a family of three daughters had spread a table with fruit, nuts, bread, butter, and a bowl of tea beside the mummified body of their mother; in 1928 a Devonshire woman sued the Paignton Urban District Council on the ground that they wrongfully obstructed her deposit of food and flowers in a vault; and in a Yorkshire seaside town before the war chocolates and sweets were weekly placed upon a grave by the mother and sister of the dead.

It is often difficult to bring new churchyards into use, no family being willing to be the first to bury its dead in them, though the old idea that the Evil One was entitled to the first one interred is probably forgotten. One churchyard has been finally "opened" by a tramp found dead in the road, and the churchyard of Bovey Tracey is said to have been long unused until a visitor's servant was buried there. Burial to the north of the church, where the ground is looked on as unconsecrated to say the least, is still infrequent. An old mourning custom still survives in the Newton Abbot district, and perhaps elsewhere. On the Sunday after the funeral the mourners wait in their pew till all others are gone, and do not talk on the way home. It has been suggested with likelihood that this is a survival of the notion that pollution attends on death, and that mourners should therefore hold themselves separate for a time.

BUSINESS AND WORK

In April, 1926, the coffin of a man drowned at Iffley was placed upon his own raft and punted down and across the Thames by bargemen, while the mourners walked along the towing-path. Had the corpse been carried across the lock, it would have had to pass along the ordinary path and through the tollgate of the landowner, Lincoln College, which does not seem to have been aware of the funeral. It was believed at Iffley, as it is all over the country, that the passage of a corpse along a footpath or through a tollgate would create a public right of way, although there is no foundation for this belief in statute law. The dead seem to have been carried feet foremost from ancient times, in order to prevent their seeing their home and door and so being able to find their way back as revenants. At the same time they were carried to burial, as a mark of honor, by the old and well-known ways and never by a new road or short-cut, even if this involved a roundabout journey. It is possible, though I do not offer it as a satisfactory explanation, that from this custom arose the complementary belief that, if the corpse did chance to travel another path, that became *ipso facto* a high road. The belief frequently crops up, and is stated to have been put forward in the High Court about 1908. When a disputed right of way over a footpath was discussed in the Godalming Council in 1910, one member inquired whether anyone knew of a corpse being carried over it, as in various northern counties this was important. He added that the moment a corpse was carried over a stile the path became an open way; owners therefore took steps to prevent such an occurrence, and in one case objection by the owner of a path leading to a burial-ground caused a corpse to be taken five miles round a mountain from an outlying farm. However this may be, we have here an example of a whole body of folk custom and belief which is looked on as having the force of law and yet differs from statute law. Here are other examples:

Until the worry was got rid of by forming new parishes upon the growth of population, the parishes of Walthamstow and Leyton were embarrassed by a "Walthamstow strip" which ran right across Leyton from the Lea to the Snaresbrook, parallel with the southern boundary of Walthamstow. About this the story is that Leyton parish had once refused to bury a person drowned in the Lea. Walthamstow buried the body, and so became entitled to take from Leyton a strip of land, right across, as broad as the corpse-bearers could cover, walking hand in hand, with arms extended. Disputes between parishes as to the burial of bodies still persist. In 1926 a dead girl baby was found at the water's edge at Sandgate, which parish extends only to high-water mark, below which the foreshore is still in the parish of Cheriton, two miles inland. As the body lay below the mark, the latter parish had to bear the cost of burial. The folk attach great importance to the right of burial in relation to property. At Chepstow in 1914 three parties fought for possession of the coffin of an old age pensioner, believing that to secure it would give the right to bury the corpse and hence to inherit the property of the dead.

I find the belief strong that all persons born of English parents at sea belong to the parish of Stepney. This old folk notion once found its way into the courts. A Cheshire magistrate sent a wanderer to Stepney as "born at sea," and successful legal action was taken by the London parish. It is still believed in several districts that, according to manorial custom, if a house can be built on common land, covered, and a pot boiled therein or at least smoke sent out of its chimney, all between sunset and sunrise, the ground on which it stands becomes the property of the builder. Local customs also exercise considerable unofficial control over marital offenses. This is certainly useful, for some regard their home duties in the same way as a man who was recently bound over at Lambeth Police Court to keep the peace towards his wife, and asserted: "I assaulted my wife because I thought, as a man, I was in duty bound to do so." The ceremonies by which the folk intervenes, now as in the past, in cases of offenses against morality or arising from what old Gerarde terms "woman's willfulness in stumbling upon their hasty husbands' fists," go by different names in different localities, such as "riding the stang" (Lines), "ran-tanning" (Notts), "skimity" or "skimmington riding" (Devon), "loobelling" (Warwick), "tin-kittlein" (Middlesex), and "wooset hunting" (Hants). In general a procession ends with the chanting of appropriate verses before the offender's door, to the accompaniment of "rough music" from tin cans, tongs, and other improvised instruments, and effigies are sometimes burnt or buried. For wife-beating chaff is strewn on the threshold "to show that he'd bin a-threshin'," and the woman who has beaten her man has her roof covered with straw. It is a firm conviction that these practices are perfectly legal so long as they are gone through for three successive nights and, sometimes, if the procession winds round the village church. Locally the performance may take place on three nights, then there is an interval of three nights, and so on until there have been nine celebrations in all.

When local opinion decides that a wife has been absent from home longer than is justifiable, a broom, decorated with ribbon, will be hung over the doorway, or stuck in a chimney or window, as an advertisement for a housekeeper. When the man himself puts out the broom, it is understood that he invites his friends to carouse with him during the housewife's absence, the broom, in this case, being equivalent to the bush (the old sign of an inn), the putting out of which some still vaguely think would entitle anyone on the fair day to sell beer and wine without a license. Another folk custom, evolved to meet a practical difficulty and to permit a legal-seeming separation from board and bed in days when Church and State alike forbade divorce, is that of wife-selling, an old foreign reproach to the British nation, which is not merely a tradition utilized by Thomas Hardy in *The Mayor of Casterbridge*, but is far more common than is supposed. The sale is imagined to be legal if the price is not less than a shilling and if the woman is handed over with a halter round her neck (apparently to show that she is property to be disposed of like haltered cattle);

the woman must also not be resold to a third party by her purchaser. It has been suggested that the idea of the legality of the transfer was much strengthened by the number of soldiers who returned from the wars against France over a century ago, to find that false reports of their deaths had deceived their wives into remarriage. They could not afford the great cost of legal action, and the authorities considered the cases too numerous for interference, so the position was "regularized" by a great revival of the old custom of wife-selling.

A number of examples of formal wife-transfer have been noted since the war, and a great many before it, and it seems worth while to quote samples clearly established by reports of evidence in court, and probably a very small fraction of the actual total. The wives were generally consenting parties, and some of them preserved the receipts for themselves as a proof of their "respectability." I cannot resist taking, first of all, a pre-war case, because it happened, of all places, at Dunmow (of the Flitch of Bacon). In 1908, in a court charge that a woman had been ill-treated and turned out with her two youngest children, it came out that she had been bought for £5 from her husband in 1880 and had borne twelve children to the buyer.

In 1919 a woman coolly stated to the Tottenham magistrates that her husband had given her away to another man. In 1920 it was in evidence in the Southend Police Court that a husband had persuaded a man to sign a document in a teashop, agreeing to take over the wife and look after her. In 1924, during the hearing at Newcastle-on-Tyne of a charge of persistent cruelty against a fruit salesman, his wife gave evidence that she had found in her husband's pocket a signed agreement to take over "with all appurtenances" the wife of another man. At the Devonshire Assizes in 1926, in a divorce case, mention was made of an offer to buy the wife. It will be appreciated that divorce proceedings are, to the poor, even yet incomprehensible in their technicalities, as well as costly, and that a bargain to sell, with money passing, will prevent a suit. The Leeds magistrates in 1926 had evidence before them of the sale of a wife for £10, apparently with her full consent. In May, 1928, evidence was given before the magistrates at Blackwood (Mon.) that a wife was sold for £1 by her husband, who gave a written document to the purchaser, and, in reply to the court, said that he did not sell his baby "because it was my own flesh and blood."

The idea that a wife was leased and could be sold like other leaseholds has been sometimes expressed even more clearly by additions to a simple sale. She has been led, haltered, through a turnpike gate, and toll paid for her as for farm stock, or she has been put up for auction, haltered, in open market. In Shropshire it was thought, not so long ago, that if a husband failed to support his wife she might give back her ring and then be free to remarry. Many other examples could be given of customary law followed by the folk. In most places they do not regard promises as more than piecrust unless these are made formal by some ceremony, such as by "wetting" with a drink or by giving "earnest money," like the "King's shilling" to an Army recruit; the "earnest" is needed "to bind the bargain" with a farm laborer at the "statty" or statutory fair at which he is hired- known as the "fessen-penny" or fasten-penny in Lincolnshire. In London, more perhaps than elsewhere, there is a belief, held without repugnance, that incurables, and especially those suffering from hydrophobia, are smothered after the King's consent has been obtained.

Nor is this all. There are distinct traces yet remaining of a social order not that of the present day or of the feudal system, but one of communal ownership of land and boats and gear under "unwritten" laws. Scholars, especially of late years, have tended to refer the basis of our English institutions more and more ultimately back to Rome, but folklore finds much surviving from other and older sources. As a summary in outline I quote, by permission, two paragraphs from Mr. F. M. Stenton's account in *The Handbook of Folklore*:

"At every period of English history, from the Anglo-Saxon Conquest to the agrarian revolution which marks the close of the eighteenth century, the basis of the national life was supplied by the village community, and the agricultural system of which it was the expression. The normal village was planted at a junction of roads, towards the center of a wide expanse of arable land; and it was in the treatment of the arable that the features characteristic of early methods of cultivation were most clearly manifested. The rudimentary nature of current agricultural practices rendered it necessary that no portion of the arable land should bear crops for more than two years in succession; and in the larger part of England a traditional rotation was established by which, in each year, one-third of the arable lay fallow. In the following season the same tract of land would be sown with wheat; a year later it would bear peas or beans. The result of this custom was that the whole of the arable land within the village territory in due course underwent a period of fallow; and, upon the fallow, the cattle within the village were depastured according to rules determined by the common consent of the whole community. Each of the three large 'fields' into which the village land thus fell was divided into a vast number of strips or 'lands' of unequal area, defined either by a bulk of unplowed turf or by a vacant furrow. Within the same field single strips might well vary from half a rood to an entire acre or more. The plotting of these strips, a work accomplished in an age of incalculable antiquity, was determined by the natural drainage of the soil; the complex plan of an open field can only be understood in relation to the contour of the ground. Groups of strips naturally connected were known as furlongs, and frequently bore the name of some early settler of local prominence. Along the heads of the strips ran vacant 'lands' used for turning the plow; they were called 'headlands,' and their direction is marked, even at the present day, by the irregular course of countless English lanes."

The Hertfordshire Ancient Monuments Inventory shows Bygrave, Clothall, and Wallington as unenclosed parishes, with enclosed pastures immediately round the medieval vills, and, beyond these, great arable fields without hedges, and divided, as described by Mr. Stenton, by turf balks. The arable of Clothall is as much as 600 acres. It has been pointed out that, to allow these surrounding stretches of unenclosed arable, many villages on their original sites are situated a little way from the ancient main roads. The open fields system at Upton St. Leonard's (Gloucestershire) lasted until 1897.

Much of this ancient system and its customary law was to be found surviving in the manorial courts and court leets, which as real working bodies came to an end in 1926 as a consequence of the Law of Property Act of 1925. Before that date a considerable number met regularly for business, and others on special occasions- e.g., the Court of Shepway of the Cinque Ports, 800 years old, met in 1923 on the site of the old Shepway Cross, near Lympne. The courts certainly embalmed practices and ideas of Anglo-Saxon date, if not still earlier, which had been first modified to fit into the feudal system in Norman times and had then been shorn, little by little, by statute law of their functions of dealing, quite apart from King and Parliament, with a wide range of local affairs. The subject is too large for detailed treatment here, and has received a good deal of attention from both serious student and curiosity-monger.

The latter has pleased himself with such strange vagaries as the "Whispering Court" of Rochford Manor (Essex), which met on the Wednesday midnight after Michaelmas Day in the open air on King's Hill, no one speaking above a whisper and a piece of coal being used for recording. The "quit" or customary rents paid for a very large number of properties are often of a jocular or trivial character, which is sometimes due to changed times; one made most familiar by annual newspaper description and illustration is paid by the City of London, the home of innumerable ancient customs, which for 700 years or so has, towards the end of October, rendered to the King's Court of

Exchequer (but of late to the King's Remembrancer) two faggots, a billhook and a hatchet (replacing two knives), six horseshoes, and sixty-one nails, with accompanying ceremonial, as quit rents for a piece of land now covered by the Law Courts, and another piece in Shropshire, the whereabouts of which is unknown. An eminent French folklorist, M. Sebillot, published in 1895 a volume on *Legendes et curiosites des metiers*, and some collection of the folklore of industries has been made in Germany and a few other countries. But, so far as I am aware, apart from the contents of Sir James Frazer's vast and worldwide record of the ways of husbandmen and various others in *The Golden Bough*, very little has been done to collect the folklore of English occupations. A little space will therefore be spared here to draw attention to the richness of the land which may be possessed and its harvests reaped by the student.

Of agriculture, the most conservative of all in its traditions and gear, a few illustrations may suffice. The ancient custom of gleaning has almost gone, but there is a sense of grievance left behind, as the people feel that by customary law it should be perfectly legal. The claim of right to glean has twice been brought before the High Court. One action succeeded, and the appellants claimed the support of Blackstone and Hale, but it was finally held by three judges that the custom had no foundation in law, interfered with the enjoyment of property by owners, and conduced to vagrancy and other mischiefs. Flails are still used for threshing in Essex, and special forms of the notched sticks (either natural round sticks with the bark on or squared lengths of wood) known as "tallies" (which were once stored as records of the national accounts in the Chancellor's bag or "budget") are employed for counting sheep and lambs on the South Downs, or for quantities of hops. Another custom supposed by many to be extinct is far from being so, parish land being let in many cases by candle auction.

In one form, an inch of candle is cut off, and the meadow

is let to the last bidder as the candle inch flickers out, which in one case in 1927 took an hour and a quarter. A field of seven acres was let in 1919 in this way at Chard (Somerset), and the parish field at Grimston, near Melton Mowbray, in 1926, but only half an inch was used to let for twenty-one years the "Church Ale" land in 1925 at Chedzoy, near Bridgwater. Another method adopted is to light a wax candle and thrust in a pin one inch below the flame, the bidding ending when the pin drops out. This seems to be the more usual form of the auction, as I have notes of it within the last few years at Aldermaston near Reading, Broadway in Dorset, Butterwick near Boston, and various places in Berks, Devon, Somerset, etc. A modernization is followed at Asfordby (Leicestershire), where the parish field was let in 1926 "by watch," the bidding being stopped at the end of three minutes. The annual hiring-times of farm servants differ according to the county- e.g., Michaelmas in Hants, May and Martinmas in Derbyshire, Yorkshire, and the north of England, and Christmas in North-East Shropshire, Cheshire, and West Staffordshire. In North Northumberland working stewards and shepherds are engaged at the new year, but do not enter on their work until "May Day," which means May 12 (Old May Day)- one of many instances of adherence to the Julian Calendar, which was officially superseded in 1752. No notice is taken in this district of May 1, May Day in our present calendar, and the men, women and girl workers are engaged at annual hirings in the first week of March. Many farming festivals have disappeared within living memory. At sheep-shearing there is no longer a gathering of the neighborhood to assist, and the work is done by machine, but the old social institution is often remembered by giving a glass of wine or mug of cider to all visitors "to drink to the health of the flock." I have been told that it is not yet wholly forgotten that a lock of wool should be put in a shepherd's coffin, of which the purpose seems to have been to supply him with proof on Judgment Day of his calling, and thus to excuse his remissness in attendance at church.

Some folklore of the dairy industry was noted by the

medical officer of health in a report on the Freebridge Lynn Rural District (West Norfolk), quoted in The Eastern Daily Press about twenty years ago. Throughout the whole district, he says, it was believed that, unless the hands of the milker were washed both before and after milking, the cow would become dry. Milk must always be kept quiet, and so the dairy door was never slammed. If any milk were spilled upon the cow's legs, in milking, the cow would become dry. When a cow was milked, the first few drops were used to moisten the palm of the milker's hand, for it was not well to milk "with a dry hand" (a piece of sympathetic magic). Before milking, a few drops were milked upon the ground, professedly to wash out the duct, and the last drops in the pail were also thrown away. However matted a cow's tail might be, it must never be cut with a sharp instrument, as the cow would then abort her calf.

In occupations involving uncertainty of outlook, naturally much attention is given to matters thought likely to give protection and luck. The sailor thinks it the worst of luck to have a coffin or corpse on board, and, perhaps from association with the burial service and black clothes, a parson is almost as unwelcome. "Here's a parson; he hasn't paid for his washing," was told to me on shipboard as a well-known sailors' saying, with a harrowing account of the "dirty weather" on an earlier voyage with a certain bishop on board. Whistling, or driving a nail into the mast, brings wind. It is a common notion that ships with a name ending in "a" (such as Lusitania), or whose name has been changed, are doomed thereby to ill-luck (probably reinforced in the Navy by the loss of the Cobra and Victoria, to which both objections applied). There is also a belief that a sailing ship without a figure-head cannot sink; after repeated failures to sink the schooner Amy off Portland to provide a scene for a film dealing with "Q" mystery ships in the recent war, she was thought by old salts to be hoodooed, and her figure-head was restored before she finally went under in March, 1928. Various animals bring bad weather with them on board, and pigs must on no account be named on a tug. The drowning of the ship's cat makes disaster certain, and she "carries a gale in her tail." "Rats leave a sinking ship" has become a general proverb. Disaster is coming if anything unnatural happens, such as the appearance of a land bird on board at sea. These beliefs are not without their serious practical effects. In 1923 a sailor was charged at Grimsby with refusing to join his ship, which was lying waiting in the river, and he explained that it was bad luck to join after the ship had sailed.

In April, 1927, the bodies of a Norwegian captain and four sailors were found on the shore near Bude, and could not have been in the water long. According to a newspaper report, a farmer's wife living near the beach thought that she heard moans during the night, but made no search as she was satisfied with the suggestion that it must be the wind or the "Devil's Sailor." The latter is said to be seen at full moon, and to haunt a cave in which he was chained by the Devil, who was angered by the man's efforts to escape and suicide; the Devil promised him freedom when he had made a rope from sand. Fishermen have naturally a great regard for weather omens and for lucky and unlucky signs. They believe that the moon governs the weather, and in Northumberland bad weather is expected if the new moon falls on Friday. A seagull flying against the window brings warning of danger to one of the family at sea. On one part of the East Coast, fishermen's wives will not wind wool after sundown, lest, if they do, they will soon be making their husbands' shrouds. Unlucky boats, from which some of the crew have been lost, will even be burnt. Rabbits must not be named on board, nor a hatch cover turned upside down, and in Northumberland the name "Graham" must not be spoken. To insure a good catch, the sign of the cross is made over the nets before fishing. Tea-leaves are "read" with special meanings- e.g. an "oar" warns to be cautious when embarking, "lily" is good fortune, and so on.

The mining industry has its own peculiar customs. In 1920, when there was a strike of miners in Derbyshire, the men prospected among the derelict lead-mines, of which one estimate says there are 4,000 in ten square miles of the Matlock district. They found a workable vein in an old shaft abandoned probably for three centuries near Oaker Hill at Wensley, and in accordance with customary law the ownerless Barley Close mine was handed over to the finders by the Barmaster. Anyone can claim an unworked mine and, by paying a fee of not more than 25s., can become its owner. As the price of lead had risen greatly, many claims of this kind were made- e.g., to the Plackett mines at Winster and to the Wraith mines at Elton. In February, 1920, an interesting further point was raised of mining custom. A miner had acquired, in the way described above, the Portoway mines at Winster, and claimed access by roadway, which was denied by the owner of the surface soil. Ancient custom allows that, when a mine is in actual working, land can be taken, without payment, for a roadway to the nearest watercourse for washing the ore and to the nearest King's highway for its transport. The King's Barmaster for the High Peak Hundred, with two grand jurymen, on the miner's appeal, formally handed over the right of way sought. The Barmaster, with a grand juryman on either side, with his arms fully outstretched, paced over the ground, and a road was staked out between the lines traced by the outside finger-tips of the grand jurymen.

Besides their codes of customary laws, the miners have much other folklore, and the older generation still believes in the "knockers" and other supernatural beings haunting the mines (see Chapter VI). Great regard is paid to omens, and many things are prohibited for fear of ill luck following them. Thus, in 1920 the Halesowen Colliery near Birmingham was "standing" for two days, and large ironworks dependent on it were closed for three days, as the miners ceased work after one had been killed, for fear that ill-luck would follow the non-payment of this mark of respect. The collier, and not in all cases the older man only, will turn back if on his way to work he meets a woman. Although cleanly enough otherwise, he refuses to wash his back more than, say, once a week, as he thinks that it will have a weakening effect. The most curious recent mining "custom" I have encountered is in the report of a local newspaper in 1911, when seventeen colliery horse drivers were summoned for neglect of work by the Stourbridge Glazed Brick and Fireclay Company, the owners of the Corbyn's Hall Colliery, Pensnett, near Dudley. In 1910 the colliery became very wet owing to the heavy rains, and the manager raised the men's wages 4d. a day on their complaint. On February 23, 1911, however, the men refused to go down the shaft. The manager gave evidence that he saw them, and that they resorted to an old custom and threw a brick in the air. If it came down again they would have a holiday, but if it remained in the air they would go to work. The brick seems to have fallen, and the court ordered the men to pay the Company the amount claimed and costs. Much might have been added concerning the special folklore of other risky industries and of the gambler, burglar, boxer, sportsman, and soldier, and of the stage. The last named has many interesting taboos. The last lines (or "tag") of a piece must not be spoken at rehearsal, luggage must go in a dress-basket and not in a trunk with nails, real flowers must not be used nor an umbrella opened on the stage, green and black ought never to be worn, whistling in a dressing-room is improper, and to quote or perform Macbeth is very unlucky.

But the less dangerous or uncertain trades have also plenty of folklore, and it is to be noted that industries of recent date are as well provided as those of ancient date, and even, as in the case of printing with its "chapel," have evolved a trade guild. If we take the comparatively recent art of dressmaking, we find that to jump over a dress when finished is a certain means of preventing its return for alterations. Dressmakers will not fit with black pins, nor tack with green thread. Care is taken not to bring bad luck on a bride by staining the bridal dress with blood from a pricked finger. "Unpick on Monday and you unpick all the week." It is a sign of the worker's own wedding coming soon if she accidentally sews one of her own hairs into a garment of a trousseau.

If by chance, in trying on, a new garment is pinned to the customer's other clothes, it is reckoned that each pin so attached means that a year will elapse before her marriage.

In tailoring, the cloth left over from the making of a suit is a perquisite, and is spoken of as "cabbage." In 1921 it was stated in the Clerkenwell County Court that it was the custom in the trade for a workman to hand over his scissors to his employer when he was engaged, as a guarantee that he would turn up at the time appointed. To close the chapter, we will mention what looks like a survival in what was once the serious trade of archery. At the annual archery meeting of the Woodmen of Arden (held in 1927) at Meriden in Warwickshire, the marker signals a bull by dancing a jig, and a "clout" in the very center by lying on his back and waving his legs.

ENGLISH FOLKLORE

CALENDAR CUSTOMS

"Ye Merrie England of ye Olden Time" of stage and story, with its folk chiefly engaged in dancing around the maypole on the village green or dragging the yule log into the baronial hall, according to the season of the year, is the creation of the romanticists and poets and painters of the nineteenth century, and is, in truth, an incomplete and even misleading picture of the past. The man-in-the-street knows something about "going a-maying" in "the merry month of May," and is pleased "to remember the fifth of November"; but he knows little of the dreary background, of town and country life alike, in medieval and early England, which made people plunge boisterously into the celebrations of the festivals fixed by particular days and seasons in the calendar. The roadways, well nigh impassable in winter, made communication difficult between village and village, while the nights were ill-lighted and haunted by fearsome bogles, ghosts, and witches. The communal farming already mentioned laid down a monotonous trivial round and daily task of life. The food was not varied as it is today. Hay was not made and stored, and cattle and pigs were slaughtered at the beginning of winter, wherein scurvy and other ailments arose from a diet largely of salted meat. Little wonder, then, if the annual fair, generally held on the Sunday after the day of the saint to whom the village church was dedicated, was a time of reaction and merrymaking, and the other calendar festivals, both the twelve days of Christmastide and the other greater festivals, and the smaller ones of souling, catterning, elementing, Thomasing, and the rest, were eagerly looked forward to and anxiously enjoyed. The greater district fairs, too, had an industrial importance beyond that of being, as to a less extent they are now, occasions of hiring servants, and markets for disposing of cattle, sheep, and pigs, for at them were bought the stocks of provisions and necessaries for the long months of winter and foul weather.

But these once general festivals have very greatly

diminished in popularity since the first quarter of the nineteenth century. Indeed, with the accelerated disuse which set in with the war, some are quite or almost gone. Guy Fawkes' day, in London especially, has begun to be merely one night of several- stretching last year to nearly a fortnight- on which are let off fireworks, no longer home made, and the "guys" are becoming meaningless effigies, of no one in particular, paraded about as an excuse for begging money, and in most cases without subsequent bonfires for their burning. No branch of folklore has decayed so much in recent years as calendar customs. Those familiar to me in my own boyhood- the local fair where I spent the pennies painfully saved up for a twelvemonth, the making of "April fools" by inviting attention to things which were not there, by imaginary errands, or other hoaxes before noon on the first of April, the demand to "show your rump" (spray of oak-leaves) on Royal Oak Day (May 29), the mutual sharing of Spanish-juice (licorice) water on Palm Sunday (the water coming from certain springs), and other rites in my natal district- "all, all are gone, the old familiar faces."

It ought not to be inferred from the above that the disappearance has been complete in every district, nor that many practices supposed by the writer to be extinct are not yet lingering in corners unknown to him, or have revived in favoring local circumstances. While festivals once widespread have faded, others appealing to local pride have persisted in full vigor or been restored to life, and a few new ones seem possible candidates for the succession to old ones. Instances will be given presently. Most details of the greater festivals are set out in the easily accessible volumes of Brand, Hone, and Chambers, and what follows should be understood to be no more than a sample selection from bulky notes of customs which have been in use within the last few years.

"Firstfooting" has no longer its ancient importance, but in many neighborhoods, mainly in the North, the luck of the coming year is still held to depend on the first to enter the house after midnight on December 31. A woman in this, as in so many other matters, brings ill-luck, but there is the oddest difference between places close together as to whether the man who enters should be dark or fair, towns ten miles apart in Lancashire having these opposites. A careful collection and mapping of these variations would give interesting results. The firstfooter should generally, in the Midlands, be a bachelor. He must bring something in with him, often a lump of coal or something dark if he is himself dark, but properly salt, coal, bread, and a coin. Sometimes he is preferred to have the high arched instep under which water can flow, which (as noted in chapter nine of Charlotte Bronte's Shirley) is the mark that there has been no slave in the family for three centuries. The Christian name of the incomer is significant, as, he being the first person of the opposite sex seen in the new year, it is the same as that of the future husband of the lass who lets him in. In some parts of Yorkshire the "lucky bird" lets Christmas in. What is done on New Year's Day will be done all the year, and there was an instance in 1926 in the West Country of refusal to work on that day lest it should result in hard work all the year long. On this day also in Devon, for luck all the year, soup is made with whole peas, as split peas would split the luck.

On Plow Monday, the first Monday after Old Christmas Day (January 6), in a few places farm laborers decorate themselves with ribbons and mask or blacken their faces; they sing and dance, for money and beer, in houses to which they are admitted, but seem no longer to carry with them a plow wherewith to plow up the doorsteps of those who refuse to give. Rarely a mumming play is performed by them. One of the rhymes still chanted by boys in Bucks on this day, to an accompaniment on tin trays, sticks, etc., sets out the meaning:

"O, O, E, I, O,
Up with the shovel and the hoe,
Down with the fiddle and the drum.
No more work for poor old neddy.
Now that the plowing's done."

Valentine's Day (February 14) has now little observance, but it is believed that birds then mate. The children of Chipping Norton (Oxon) as late as 1923 serenaded the local tradespeople with valentine doggerel, and scrambled for their gifts. "Valentine, bishop and martyr," was omitted from the calendar of the Church of England as revised in 1927, and was not restored thereto on further revision, as were SS. Crispin and Crispinian, St. Denys, St. Nicholas (Santa Claus), and St. Catherine of Alexandria (of the wheel), perhaps mythical but richly symbolic figures. The costly gifts of the days of Samuel Pepys, when valentines were assigned by drawing lots, were succeeded early in the nineteenth century by hand paintings and verses framed in their boxes by paper lace, the fashion for which culminated about sixty years ago and was probably ended by the vulgar "long valentine" with coarse pictures and abusive text which filled shops in poor neighborhoods. In the last two years an attempt has been made to revive valentines and valentine gifts, with some success.

Shrove Tuesday has its ancient pancakes, originally a means of using up all dripping and lard before Lent. In a few villages the first batch of hot pancakes is thrown into the chicken run, to insure a future abundance of eggs. At Olney (Bucks), when the "pancake bells" are rung, the womenfolks of the ringers race to the church with pancakes for their men. The pancake bell is rung in many places. In 1928 the Prince of Wales started the annual Shrove Tuesday rough-and-tumble football contest at Ashbourne (Derby) between Uptowners and Downtowners, the water goals being three miles apart. Such struggles on this day were once very common, and survive in the streets of Atherstone (Warwick) and at Alnwick and Doncaster. From the accompaniments in other countries it seems to be the remains of a rite for promoting-fertiHty. The annual scramble in Westminster School for a pancake tossed over a screen by the cook is a familiar newspaper item. On the day following, "Fritter Wednesday," fritters (or small pancakes with apples or currants) are made in the North.

ENGLISH FOLKLORE

"Hallaton bottle-kicking" is a Leicestershire contest at the beginning of April somewhat like the football mentioned above. After two veal-and-bacon pies have been scrambled for, the villagers of Hallaton and Melbourne strive to get two large brass-bound wooden beer bottles over a stream which is the common boundary of the two parishes. The victors, it is said, had once charge of a charity now lost, and the expenses are a burden on land known as Harecrop Leys. (The pies were formerly of hares.)

Mid-Lent Sunday (the fourth) was the day on which offerings were made at the high altar of the mother-church, and, derived from this, visits were, and are, paid to parents on this "Mothering Sunday." While special "mothering cakes" are made for gifts on this day, its origin is yet so forgotten in some quarters that a prominent English weekly permitted itself recently to write that the idea of a "Mother's Day" originated in America twenty years ago, and had been "adopted" in England! "Mothering Sunday" is also "Simnel Sunday," when simnel cakes are eaten in Lancashire. Palm Sunday in the heavy woolen district of the West Riding is "Toffee Sunday," when even old people munch that dainty; and elsewhere it is "Fig Sunday." "Palms" (willow or yew) are worn in many country places.

Good Friday is a day on which many things are proper to be done, from playing marbles in a Sussex village to the performance, by boys with swords of lath and decorated coats and pasteboard hats, in a part of the West Riding, of the old folk play St. George and the Dragon, or The Peace Egg. In the West Country, clothes must on no account be washed, nor a child weaned, nor finger-nails cut, but everywhere it is the lucky day for planting potatoes- "You never get any good potatoes unless you plant on Good Friday"- and for other garden work. Hot cross buns are, of course, as popular as ever. Easter is the ancient spring festival well observed, though the significant customs of the men "heaving" or lifting the women on Easter Monday, and the women the men on the following day, are only observed as an occasional frolic. The filling of artificial Easter eggs with gifts is no older than 1870; the first case of toys received from Paris after the raising of its siege was a collection of Easter eggs, and the costliness of the contents has grown until in 1924 one freak Easter egg contained jewels to the value of £7,000. The egg and hare imported by fashion have not killed the home-dyed folk egg and the sports of egg-jarping and egg-rolling in the North.

In the former, hard-boiled eggs are struck against each other, and the owner of the victor annexes the cracked egg, a custom widespread over Europe. In the latter, dyed eggs are raced by rolling them down slopes. At Avenham Park, Preston, 50,000 people gathered on Easter Monday, 1927, in order to fight battles and run races with eggs. Easter Sunday is "Sugar-Cup Sunday" in Derbyshire, because the children go a round of wells and streams with cups and sugar, and wish while they drink sugar-water. It is universally thought that it is necessary to wear something new on this day, or very bad luck will follow. It is the occasion of many local celebrations, such as the distribution of memorial "rolls" (biscuits) and bread and cheese under the will of the Biddenden maids (Kent), chiefly curious for the local story which makes the sisters Siamese twins because they are so represented on the biscuits which are given away- a tradition, some say, with no other basis than the way in which an early baker tried to picture two damsels side by side on one narrow biscuit.

Following the second Sunday after Easter comes Hocktide, the Tuesday of which is "kissing day" at Hungerford (Berks), one of the last two unreformed boroughs, with a constitution presenting many ancient features. It appoints, in place of mayor and corporation, a constable, port reeve, bailiff, and other officials, including two tithingmen or tutti (pretty) men. On Hockney Day (Hock Tuesday) the tutti men, each carrying a pole decorated with a bouquet and tipped with an orange, and followed by a man loaded with oranges, perambulate the place, claiming a "head-penny" from every man and a kiss from every woman. An orange is offered to every person kissed, from the poles, and at the evening dinner the toast is drunk, in solemn silence, of John of Gaunt, who, as engraved on the ancient horn of summons, "did give and grant the Royal fishing in Hungerford town." Hocking means "lifting," and Hocktide must at some former period have had "lifting" customs like those at Easter. May Day is still one of the great annual festivals, though now in the towns it is rather "Labor Day" and the time for cart-horse parades and decoration than for the ancient rites and sports, which have become child's play rather than a national celebration. In the villages and some small towns little girls carry round "garlands," usually in the shape of a hoop or of two hoops fixed crosswise, and often with a doll suspended in the middle; they sing May Day songs. May queens, in several cases instituted through the influence of John Ruskin, are to be found here and there. A very few maypoles survive, and some have been erected in recent years. Even gathering May dew for the complexion is not unknown. Some little of ancient rites is probably embodied in the proceedings on "Garland Day" (May 29) at Castleton (Derby). Here an enormous floral crown is carried in procession on the shoulders of a mounted man, followed by dancers and a "Bessy" (man in woman's dress) of the kind usual in Morris dances; the garland is hoisted on the church tower. The whole seems to be a transfer in the seventeenth century from May Day to Restoration Day.

Rogationtide, the week including Ascension Day, has seen a considerable revival since the war both of religious services to bless crops, flocks, and fishing, and of the ceremonies of "beating the bounds" of parishes, which served formerly the twofold purpose of blessing the land (as indicated by the "Gospel oaks" upon the boundaries, where Scripture passages were read aloud) and of keeping in memory the true boundaries and discovering encroachments and obstructions. Such annual action was particularly necessary where the ancient communal ownership and open fields persisted. In 1924, in the riding of the bounds by the inhabitants of Longhorseley (Northumberland), a fence put up on enclosed common ground was pulled down. Examples of revival of the custom of beating the bounds, which has continued without break in a large number of places, are: East Barnet in 1925, after a gap of sixty odd years; Datchet (Bucks) in 1925, after twenty-one years; St. Clement's parish, Hastings, in 1923, seven years; Bexhill in 1925, after sixteen years. Perhaps the most picturesque survival today is at Hunmanby, on the Yorkshire coast, where, to define the limits of the manor, after three casts of a trawl net a man rides into the sea as far as possible and then casts a javelin out to sea. The boundaries are impressed on the minds of either children or adults by "bumping" or "dunting" them on salient points such as boundary stones, or by supplying the children with peeled wands wherewith to strike the landmarks. At Poole Harbor in 1925 the boys were whipped with bootlaces and the girls pricked with hairpins (apparently still surviving at Poole). On Ascension Day the "dressing" takes place of the five wells at Tissington and of the wells at some other places in Derbyshire. The pictures and designs formed on clay-covered boards with a mosaic of flowers, leaves, and berries are very pretty, but the claim to great antiquity of the custom is doubtful.

Enough has been written to direct attention to the variety and number of the folk customs and beliefs clustering round the present-day calendar. The calendar itself would repay our study, with its double system of movable feasts all dependent on the "ecclesiastical" (and not astronomical) moon of Easter, and fixed feasts based on a solar calendar. It would be interesting, also, to examine why some customs are still hale and hearty and others disappearing; for example, elementing (the celebration of the Feast of St. Clement, or Old Clem, the blacksmith's patron) has failed with the dying out of the blacksmith's craft itself from lack of apprentices. The long procession of other festivals- to name only Royal Oak Day, Whitsuntide, Midsummer Eve and Day, Harvest, the Days of SS. Barnabas, Swithin, James, Clement, Catherine, and Thomas and others, Michaelmas, All Hallowe'en, Fifth of November with its burning of the old year, Martinmas, Holy

Innocents' Day (the unluckiest of all the year), with other ancient calendar survivals such as the election of mock mayors and a boy bishop, and the crowning winter festival of Christmas- would need a whole volume merely to outline their living folklore. I cannot, however, resist mention of one rather pathetic survival in London about the end of July- viz., "Grotto Day" (or, rather, two or three days). In 1927 the boys' "grottoes," for which they begged "only a ha'penny," had sunk in South London to little enclosures outlined on the pavement with moss from garden walls, and generally having a cross of moss within them. Not many years ago they were substantial erections with roofs, and now and then had a lighted candle inside and a few oyster-shells outside. July 25 is the day of St. James of Compostella, and these little structures, with their oyster-shells to simulate pilgrims' scallop-shells, are the last degenerate descendants of shrines put up in London, some seven or eight centuries ago, for the comfort of those who were too poor to take the long road of pilgrimage to the popular saint's shrine in Spain.

Another instance of long endurance of old custom is in the fixing of the dates of very many village fairs by the "Old Style" Julian Calendar, which was officially abandoned in 1753, although, by the way, the nation's accounts were made up, in 1928 as in other years, to April 5- viz.. Old Lady Day- the year being reckoned from the Annunciation. Revivals of old customs have been of late remarkably numerous, and the collector of folklore ought to record carefully the dates of all such revivals, to prevent later inquiries from being misled into supposing that every detail is a copy of ancient practice, and so being drawn to false conclusions. Sometimes the revival is an utter travesty. The following are revivals during the last three or four years: "Blidworth rocking," the rocking of the last baptized infant by the vicar in an ancient cradle, bedecked with flowers and surrounded by candles, before the altar at Blidworth, near Mansfield, in February, 1923, and following years, after an interval of at least a century, the custom being alleged to go back to the thirteenth century; "clipping the church" at Wing (Bucks) in 1925; well-dressing at Buxton in 1925, and elsewhere a little earlier; the village fair at Denham, near Uxbridge, in 1925, after fifty years; the lambale at Kirtlington (Oxon) in 1925; "landing the pie" by Thomes watermen at Eel Pie Island at Twickenham in 1923, after a lapse of over a century; and the old Swainmote dinner at Mansfield (Notts), a boar's head being brought in amid garlanded and dancing girls- the dinner being once annual in connection with Sherwood Forest.

When the origins of some recent customs are forgotten, they may conceivably be regarded as ancient folk practices, and be the basis of theories of the future. The collector should therefore note their dates. For example, the hamlet of Week in Westmoreland suffered very severely from a plague of wasps in 1841. Since then it has had an annual procession to a memorial stone on the moor, and then, after a short service, a concerted attack is made on wasps and wasp nests with all manner of weapons, from insect powder onward. (Here is a germ for a theory of a wasp totem, ceremonially sacrificed by its people once a year.) Mitcham Fair (Surrey) might, with better luck, in time have established itself and become traditional; it used to be opened with a huge gilt key and a ceremony, alleging origin under Queen Elizabeth, although it had no charter and no history, but the ceremony was stopped, despite the protests of the showmen, in 1924. Six shillings "coredy money" is paid four times a year (in the first weeks of February, May, August, and November) to thirty-four poor women at Lambeth Palace; £2 each paid under a will of 1711, to boys who recite the Lord's Prayer and some other passages with their hands on a tomb at Wotton, near Dorking (typical of many like practices, the origin of which is now unknown).

Lastly, there seems to be a tendency to supplant decaying observances, such as Mothering Sunday, by artificial "days" popularized by newspapers, such as Daffodil Sunday, Bloom

Sunday (for the cherry orchards). Bluebell Sunday, Chestnut Sunday, Blackberry Sunday, Primrose Day, Empire Day, Rose Day, and Poppy Day.

ANIMALS, PLANTS, AND INANIMATE OBJECTS

When a country has been so long under civilizing influences as England has, one can hardly expect in its present-day folklore more than traces of the attitude of uncivilized races towards the animal, vegetable, and mineral kingdoms. The savage suspects life and power in them all. He worships some, and admits the equality, or even superiority, of many an individual animal, or tree, or stone, and is proud to count one of them his ancestor, relation, or protector. To him the chimpanzee is a man who is artful enough to avoid work by refusing to talk. But we must be cautious in applying savage ideas as explanations of our own folklore. The peacock is quite a modern figure in our long ages, and our dread of peacocks' feathers, especially on the stage, may not derive from an immemorial past. We need not suppose our distant forefathers to have been cat-worshipers, and to have seen the symbol of a moon goddess in waxing and waning feline eyes, because the cat walking her lone way is supposed to tell us of coming weather by turning her back to the fire or washing behind her ears, to point the direction of a coming wind with a slanted hind leg as she licks herself, to scratch "to bring down the rain," or, if she is black, to bring us luck when she enters our home or crosses our path. The cat, also, is comparatively a newcomer, although My Lord Mayor was probably much mistaken when he asserted in 1927 that she was unknown in England until two centuries after the days of Dick Whittington. Yet she has gathered much folklore around her. We drown kittens born in May in the West Country as likely to bring in snakes, and expect great good fortune when our cat sneezes the day before a wedding, but we do not require to fetch the meaning from far-off times and places. When the owl and squirrel are hunted by rustic crowds, it may be only to assert a customary right of way or common, and not a sacrificial rite.

When, however, the defendant in a cockfighting case at

Devizes in 1921 said, "I always let them (the cocks) fight until they are killed, and the one that is killed I eat, and it puts the sporting spirit into me," we find the same impulse which makes the savage eat those portions of his enemy's corpse wherein he imagines his bravery to reside.

Totemism- i.e., the belief of a social group of mankind that it is of one family with some particular class of animals, plants, or inanimate objects- is regarded by some as a stage through which practically all humanity must have passed, and it has been suggested that in England various animal surnames- e.g., Hogge, Lyon, Wolf, Catt, Salmon, Fox, Swann, Woodcock, and Partridge- and plant names e.g., Primrose, Appletree, Rose, Birch, and Beech- suggest ancient totem clans. It has also been urged that the belief that witches can turn into hares and other animals smells of totemism. (To kill a hare, by the way, in some places is expected to bring evil, probably because the animal might be a transformed human being.) But surnames are of comparatively late date, and no clear case has been made out for English totemism; so far at least as today's folklore is concerned, all can be reasonably understood without praying totemism in aid.

Many current ideas about animals are due to faulty observation or insufficient knowledge. It is not surprising that horsehairs falling into the water are believed to grow into eels and water snakes, or that live toads or frogs found in rock cavities without any visible outlet are believed to have been enclosed there when the rock itself was formed, and that decisive scientific experiments have failed to prove to the folk mind the impossibility of the survival of the batrachian for any great length of time. So vehement is the opinion that vipers swallow their young on the approach of danger, and so often has the phenomenon been said to be observed, without the production of the refugees *in situ*, that I must leave to zoologists the question whether there is here folklore or fact. The common report that hedgehogs suck cows must go into the same category.

Animals, the folk think, know many things that we do not, and are especially clever in foreseeing the coming weather. Here are some Suffolk sayings: "If you hear the sheep at night, rain is coming." "When cows lie down all facing the same way, rain is coming." "When sparrows chirrup, sure to rain." "If the rooks build high in a tree, it is a sign of a hard winter" (or, elsewhere, a hot summer). In Northumberland, if a sheep faces the wind, it is a sign of good weather. The shrew mouse will cause disease if you let it run over you, and the newt is feared, as much as ever, as dangerously venomous, and is one of the principal "animals in people's insides," said to result from the presence of their eggs or young in drinking water or food. A tale was in general circulation in 1924 of a girl who had swallowed an octopus egg, and died from the dire effects of the creature's development; readers of the newspaper report wrote that it was perfectly true and had happened in a number of different and named districts. The tale was still running in 1926.

The living folklore of birds is extensive. The pigeon, so abundant in London, is a very unlucky bird. It gives a death warning if it settles on a house. A charwoman recently saw one flying about in my garden, and said: "Send if off! If it comes down I'll wring its neck! One settled on the washhouse where I was working, and the woman's old man died." The bad luck applies to the ringdove also. Even pigeon feathers are unlucky, and in Lancashire their presence in a bed or pillow will make death a lingering one. The favored robin becomes a death omen if it approaches the window. Fowls crowding together under a bush prognosticate a quarrel and;

"A whistling maid and a crowing hen
Are neither good for God nor men,"

...but, to prevent calamity, the unfortunate imitator of the cock generally comes to an immediate and untimely end.

ENGLISH FOLKLORE

The luck of encountering a solitary magpie is even worse, but can be warded off by bowing or spitting. Every country dweller knows the saying "One for sorrow, two for mirth; three for a wedding, four for a birth," etc. The many customs connected with the cuckoo- turning money over when one first hears it, counting its notes for the number of future years of bachelorhood or maidenhood, etc. are too familiar for repetition, and so are those of the cock and of the ladybird or cowlady (no bird but a beetle, whom we implore to fly home because her house is on fire, and whose spots foretell the coming season), and the feared death's-head moth. To kill a beetle will cause rain, and the "money spider" can only be injured to one's own hurt. The folklore of eggs would fill many paragraphs. An odd number must be set under a hen (often, curiously, the otherwise unlucky number thirteen). Of the many people who break the bottom of an eggshell after the contents have been eaten, few, perhaps, remember that this was originally to prevent its use by witches.

The most important example of respect for animals is our attitude towards bees. Where the Isle of Wight disease has not emptied our hives, it is usual to "tell the bees" at least of any death in the family; a little crape bow will often be fastened on the hives so as to put them properly into mourning for the head of the family, and a little funeral cake may be crumbled on the alighting board. If not told, the bees themselves will die, and many recent instances are given. In some neighborhoods, in the North, Midlands, and South, the bees must be told personally by the heir for whom they must work in future. As the bees may swarm or leave their hives quite unexpectedly, it is thought that they are easily offended if not treated always as members of the family, and so they are at times told all important family news. At St. Briavel's (Glos), twenty five years ago, at least, the method of telling the bees of a death was to lift the hives at the moment when the corpse was lifted for its departure. If a young swarm returns to the hive, or a swarm settles on dead wood, it is a sure sign of death, and the coming of a stranger is announced in the house by the coming of a bumble bee. When a hive swarms, you may still hear the swarm "rung" or "banged" with a door-key and shovel, as otherwise it is believed that you have no right to claim it and follow it everywhere.

Turning to the plant world, of all trees the elder has the worst repute, as the tree on which Judas hanged himself, or which supplied wood for the cross, and is hence accursed. Yet you earn three years' bad luck if you cut it down. If you stand under it at sunset in Oxfordshire, you will be bewitched, and in Suffolk you will learn misfortune if you burn its "wicked wood"- perhaps a memory of its association with the ancient mother of the elves. Blackthorn is another evil tree, accursed because it flowers on Good Friday. Kissing under the mistletoe is a peculiarity of the English, whom Erasmus found to be a nation much given to kissing. But mistletoe is now rarely made, with evergreens, etc., into a proper "kissing bush." The herbs in the garden sympathize with the household. If you find sage blossoming or rosemary flourishing, then "the mistress wears the breeches," or "the missis is the master." In Monmouthshire;

"Where the mistress is the master
The parsley grows the faster."

A good housekeeper is marked by the ability to grow myrtle and thyme. You must never transplant parsley, or a member of your household will die. I have recently heard of transplanted parsley being pulled up very angrily by another person. The seed is uncertain in its germination, and the plants vanish surprisingly after the green shoots have shown themselves, having "to go down seven (or nine) times to the Devil."

The planting of potatoes, to thrive, on Good Friday has already been mentioned, and there are other local lucky dates for garden work, such as May 3 for setting kidney beans and May 7 for planting French beans. Some flowers are looked on askance.

ENGLISH FOLKLORE

The first snowdrop must not be brought into the house, and to offer the flower to the opposite sex is as much as a wish for their death. In Sussex the snowdrop is only unlucky if a solitary flower, which, if plucked and worn, brings death within a year to one of the family. In Somerset it only brings into the house ill-luck in chicken rearing. You invite death if you leave wild apple blossom or hawthorn in the house (Bucks), and it is a general idea that if your apple-tree bears blossom after fruiting it is a warning of a death in your family. In Devon the germander speedwell ("bird's eye") is not picked by school-children, as they fear that the birds would then peck out their eyes. Saffron (crocus) is believed by Cornish fishermen to bring bad luck, and saffron cake spoils the chance of a good catch. Even yet some plants are looked on, like those of fairy tale, as "life-indexes"- i.e., indicators of life or death and prosperity of some human being with whom they are linked. The "mother of thousands" is called by some Londoners "the wandering sailor." A well-educated lady said recently: "If you possess one, and any accident happens to it, be quite sure that some misfortune will befall any relative who is a sailor. It is a most unlucky plant."

Space only remains for references to sample inanimate objects. In several counties farmers and laborers affirm that stones grow and multiply, and this explanation of their appearance in the soil "stands to rayson," as the atheist said of the existence of fairies. "Puddingstone" is shown as an obvious mother-stone. A few beliefs and customs still center around stone circles, and around standing stones which turn round "when they hear the clock strike noon," or go down to drink, or are transformed men and women. A passing mention is due to our healing wells and "wishing wells" (where pins are dropped as offerings), sadly diminished in number and fame. Many wells are said to heal eye troubles, and this is the virtue of the "holy well" of "Our Black Lady of Willesden," rediscovered in 1923 in the garden of the Vicar, who pays an annual fine imposed by King Henry III for a "superstitious image" in the church, which was alleged to blink when a cure would be effected. A new healing well in Essex was also, in 1922, the scene of cures and of gatherings that were reminiscent of ancient pilgrimages. The ancient awe of moon and stars expresses itself in the respect which children are taught to pay to them by not pointing at the moon or counting stars. Seeing the new moon for the first time through glass is ominous, and a shooting star foretells death. It is firmly fixed in the folk mind that the moon presides over the weather, which changes with it, although this is not supported by observation. Before last year's eclipse a charwoman assured my wife: "The weather won't change until after the epistle" (sic). The crescent moon, as first seen after a new moon, may, of course, be either upright or lying on her back, and is expected to predict the weather for the coming month. Curiously enough, the sailor and the laborer do not agree; when the moon is upright the sailor expects, fine weather and the laborer foul. "Stand up moon, lay down sailor; lay down moon, stand up sailor." "When you see the old moon in the young moon's arms," bad weather is coming.

> "Saturday new and Sunday full.
> Never was good and never wull."

The waxing and the waning of the moon are still much regarded as, in mimetic magic, seeds are sown, trees grafted or planted, pigs killed, wood cut, and all things done during the waxing which it is desired shall increase or last longer, and during the waning all things in which the reverse effect is sought. To end on a very modern note, some women choose the time for shingling according to their belief that hair grows with the moon.

GHOSTS AND SUPERNATURAL BEINGS

Ghosts are such a matter of course to the folk that they are hardly regarded as a matter of belief. A London girl said of her country grandmother a short time ago: "My grandmother, she didn't believe in nothing, she didn't. But one night, when she was coming home with her pony and cart from market, she saw the (village) ghost. She set off home as hard as she could, but she was as white as a sheet when she got home and all trembling. But she didn't believe in nothing, she didn't."

Folklore does not cover individual experiences of the type dealt with by the Society for Psychical Research, and is not concerned with the truth or falsity of the ghostly appearances. It should take note, however, of the traditional ghosts of the countryside, and of any similar modern developments. The revenants are usually those who came to a violent end, murderers, and those who are supposed to have left worldly business unfinished and therefore to have good reason for return. A convenient way of indicating the field for investigation seems to be to comment briefly on the apparitions of which there are published reports, in the part of the Press known to me, during the last four years, and which concern no less than twenty-four counties. Many more examples would no doubt be found if local newspapers were searched, and yet the whole would probably be only a fraction of recent appearances accepted by the folk.

Three are new ghosts on traditional lines. The first is at Crumbles, near Eastbourne, where on the shingle waste the murders took place in 1920 and 1924 of Irene Munro and of Emily Bielby Kaye ("the bungalow tragedy"). A bluey-white light was said in 1924 to precede night walkers there, and there is a report that a white figure seen in 1924 was one seen a long time ago, but not for a considerable while- so that after all this may be an ancient story revived. More interesting is the story in connection with the disappearance in December, 1926, of a famous novelist. People living in the neighborhood of the lonely quarter where her abandoned car was found had, before the end of a fortnight, begun to see visions, and reported an apparition in white. Had the expectations of the local police been fulfilled, and a body found, there were all the makings of a full-blown and authenticated ghost story, which might well have been ultimately established as local tradition. In the third place, in June, 1923, there were reports of the reappearance of the "Black Lady of Windsor Castle" (said to be Queen Elizabeth), first seen in 1897.

One very curious feature in these recent ghost stories is that ghosts of antiquity and repute are in several cases said to have changed their haunts. Of three examples, the first is that recorded just before Christmas, 1926, at East Barnet, about ten miles north of London, where a night watchman reported that he had seen a clanking apparition of a skeleton in a long military cloak, identified with the ghost of a Geoffrey de Mandeville, first Earl of Essex, reputed to haunt Camlet Moat, a mile away, where he was drowned in the moat. The urban council ordered the surveyor to report if extra wages should be paid as a consequence of the watchman "for work of an exceptionally disagreeable character." The watchman who had told the story of the appearance of course denied to an inquisitive newspaper reporter that he had seen "anything out of the way," an ambiguous statement of the kind that often meets the inexperienced and too eager questioner in such cases. At East Barnet, also, folk belief is still alive as regards the Grey Lady who haunts the Grange. The second change of place is at Fenny Compton in South Warwickshire. A "ghost light," a yellow and blue ray, has been said to flit over the lonely range of hills between that village and Burton Bassett. It appeared in 1924 on the exact anniversary of its appearance in 1923, and in 1924 was said to have left its haunt in the hills to dance and caper in the churchyard. Many people have been scared by it, and say that the ghost has the traditional large eyes of fire. The suggestion that it is due to marsh gas is, of course, scouted. Warwickshire also gave, in

January, 1927, another story of a new ghost dressed in a modern nurse's uniform, but seven feet high, which caused hundreds of people to assemble at the Old Manor House, near the main street of Stourbridge. The third example is the old lady in a mob cap who has transferred herself from the village inn to the village church of Chalfont St. Peter in Buckinghamshire.

Traditional ghosts have been often seen during the chosen years- e.g., that of Cardinal Wolsey at Hampton Court Palace, where also Queen Catherine Howard and Queen Anne are said to have been seen, while Heme the Hunter is also said to have been heard near Windsor in 1926. There is a tale current at Loughton in Essex and elsewhere that Dick Turpin roasted an old woman above a fire to force her to state where her money was hidden, and is therefore doomed three times a year to ride down Trap's Hill, where the wraith of the woman leaps upon his back and the two gallop madly away, to the ill-luck of any who may chance to see them. The swirling of mists across a lonely stretch of Watling Street, near Nuneaton, has long suggested a phantom horse and rider, believed to be Dick Turpin's ghost on its way to search in the lost village of Stretton-Baskerville for bags of guineas buried there. The ghost was reported as seen walking in a three cornered hat and a coat with red sleeves by several people early in 1926, and in February, 1927, a party of motor-cyclists said that they had seen it riding across the common land. A ghost at Bere Block Dell, a copse near Emsworth in Hampshire, is referred to in correspondence in 1695 as the ghost of Catherine, Countess of Salisbury, who was beheaded upstanding on Tower Hill, as she would not stoop her head to the traitor's block. Her reappearance has been recorded at long intervals, the last time being in 1923, when she was seen by many. (The ghost has also been said to be the apparition of a man murdered when the inn was a haunt of smugglers.)

There is a long list of ghosts now credited in the London area. At Neasden, near Wembley, five miles from the Marble Arch, it was recently believed that the road between the Welsh Harp and Kingsbury is haunted. There are ghosts seen at All Hallows, Barking-by-the-Tower, and haunted houses almost by the score. The most advertised ghost is, perhaps, the Brentford Cross Roads ghost of the early part of 1926. In Kent there have been, within the last four years, ghosts alleged on Hangman's Hill; a haunted hop garden at Potkiln Farm, near Tonbridge; in 1926 a haunted manor-house near Maidstone; and a vagrant ward at Eastry, avoided by tramps as haunted. In 1926, also, a ghost seated on a white horse galloped a meadow bordering Pickhurst Hill on the road from Beckenham, and there were ghosts at Ashley Grange, near Folkestone, and Dadson House at Welling. Lancashire boasts a ghost, Lizzie from the Bolton moors, who visits the village of Withnell at the end of every Lent; visits were spoken of in 1923 and 1926. Norfolk still has a lingering belief in the Great Black Dog of Salhouse, with the fiery eye in the middle of his forehead, and in September, 1926, the ominous Brown Lady of Raynham was twice seen. The Woman in White haunting Coupland Castle, near Wooler (Northumberland), reappeared in January, 1926.

Headless ghosts of the ancient type have been seen- a woman in dazzling white in 1923 near the ruins of an old monastery (St. Helen's) between Datchet and Old Windsor (nearby which, runs the tradition, a golden carriage is hidden), and at Igtham and Fairlawne in Kent. These instances show the liveliness of the belief in ghosts and the manner in which it creates new apparitions to fill any gaps in the long procession. Usually anything that gives a shock of terror to the folk mind, such as an atrocious murder, will be likely to result in a ghostly haunting. Cornish folk were deeply impressed by the misery and sufferings of the refugees escaped to land after the sinkings by German U-boats during the war, and in 1919 the descendants of the old wreckers of that coast believed that the spirits of those drowned or shot by the submarines haunted the rocks at night, waiting to lure to destruction with false lights any passing German vessel. They were even said to have been seen making preparations for their work. But instances are known in which, perhaps for lack of better grounds, the remaining empty of a house has been enough of itself to breed a ghost story. As Dr. Johnson said of appearances after death: "All argument is against it, all belief is for it." This belief and fear is expressed in the Norfolk saying:

"From all ghoulies and ghosteses.
From all long-leggedy beasteses,
From things that go wump in the night,
Good Lord, deliver us!"

It would be difficult to treat adequately within our space the fragmentary remains of belief in other supernatural beings than ghosts to be found in current folklore. The greater pagan deities are forgotten, but the folk recollect still a few smaller beings, such as the water spirits of the Tees (Peg Powler) and Ribble (Peg-o'-Nell), and Jenny Greenteeth, who are still credited with the seizure of victims. Some recollections are hardly more than hints, like "the Old Woman" who is in charge of the cuckoos and, according to her temper at the time, releases one or two or more, brought from France, at "Heffel Cuckoo Fair" (April 14, Heathfield Fair in Sussex). Jack-o'-Lantern or Will-o'-the-Wisp is remembered, and so is the Devil, from whom many places, plants, and animals are named- e.g., the Devil's Dyke, the Devil's-bit (blue scabious), and the Devil's coachhorse (black cocktail beetle). The older Cornish miners have not forgotten the "knockers," sprites heard in the mines, and the "spriggans"; but the most remarkable news from a mining district came in April, 1926, when a "little, brown, man-like creature" was seen and handled with sticks in the Poolway Colliery of the Forest of Dean, but lost on the pit bank. A similar creature was found in a house at Coleford (Glos), crawling, but uttering no sound, in a coal scuttle. The "little man" was carried out and emptied into the drive of the house, and could not be found the next morning.

The "Gabriel hounds" or "gabble ratchets" (flocks of wild

geese or whimbrels) cause a shudder now, as formerly, when their spectral hunt sweeps overhead. Fairies are probably now lost from all but faint memory over most of England, their last appearance in Sussex being at Faygate twenty years ago. On "The Fairy Hill" at Ellingham (North Northumberland) they danced every night "until the railway was made," when they left for parts unknown. In Suffolk the fairy loaves (fossil sea-urchins) are nowadays "quite finished with; children don't go in for these." I do not know whether in the Wye Valley the "standards" (single stems at intervals left uncut in hedges and sticking up like little bushes above the remainder) are still left "for the fairies to hide in."

In Hampshire some say that apple windfalls must not be made into jelly before St. Swithin's Day, as they are not rightly apples till christened by him and are the fairies' food. But in Devonshire the pixies are yet the explanation of bewilderment out at night, only to be countered by turning the pocket or coat inside out. On New Year's Eve, 1926, a Cornish maidservant waited up until the moonlight fell upon her bedroom window, and then spread out all her money, face upwards, on the outside ledge, and left it till morning. The coins were then turned over and kissed, before bringing in, and the ceremony was expected to obtain a guarantee from the pixies of a year's good luck.

Elsewhere in England money is occasionally put out on New Year's Eve, but there is no association with the fairies, only the idea that you will then be bringing money in all the year, because what you do on New Year's Day you will do the year long. There are other instances of surviving faith in pixies, such as the dropping of pins as offerings in their haunts.

Room must be found for brief mention of "The Angels of Mons," a vision in which were embodied the appeals and hopes of exhausted and almost despairing men. Evidence favors their independence of Mr. Machen's story of "The Bowmen," and, however that may be, the English tales of St. George and his company, seen by the French as St. Michael and Joan of Arc, throw light on the folk mind. In 1917, at a time of great discouragement, a similar story of "The Angels of Essex" came from Grays and Waltham Abbey.

A third manifestation was the beating of "Drake's drum," heard by so many where no drum could be, at the surrender of the German fleet on November 21. 1918.

DIVINATION, OMENS, AND LUCK

A strange hunger to know the future is a universal human trait, and the methods of satisfying it by attempts to divine what is going to happen are not only numerous, but so familiar that little need be written about them here. The professional fortune-teller of Mayfair and the back street, who works by cards, crystal-gazing, handwriting, palmistry, astrology, psychometry, or clairvoyance, has in great part displaced home practice of the old arts, such as the rites to learn the names and persons of coming lovers and husbands on St. Agnes' Eve, Valentine's Day, Midsummer Eve, and All Hallowe'en. It is curious that the traditional rites of All Hallowe'en are better maintained in the United States than in this country. Here even tea-leaf fortune-telling has been commercialized, and one can buy cups ready marked with astrological signs or miniature playing- cards, to facilitate reading, as well as crystal balls obligingly engraved with numbers on their facets, from which fortunes can be read off from an accompanying table. There is also to be obtained a wooden model of a book, into which is screwed a metal turn-handle, so that there is a ready-made apparatus in substitution for the "Bible and key." It will be remembered that with the "Bible and key" the door-key is placed in the Gospel according to St. John or the Song of Solomon, and the Bible tied round with a garter from the left leg, so that it can be suspended by resting the key ring upon the fist or upon two wedding fingers. A passage is repeated- e.g., Song of Sol. Viii. 6-7- and then the alphabet, the key and Bible twisting when the initial letter is reached of the name desired. To detect a thief, the key wards must rest against the words of Ps. 1. 18, and the verses should be repeated before each name of a suspect is spoken. With the "shop" apparatus it is only necessary to repeat the alphabet, and all the mystic thrill is lost.

Another commercialized divining means is that for the detection of the sex of the unborn, which was shown to a doctor friend billeted in Norfolk during the war. His landlady wanted to separate hen eggs for setting from cock eggs for immediate consumption, and suspended a small cork by a thread held between thumb and forefinger over the egg to be tested. The sex was announced by the cork oscillating from side to side or moving in a circle. She said the pendulum would only indicate sex for certain people, and, in reply to a question put some time afterwards, said that the selection had succeeded "fairly." This method of divination is now chiefly practiced as a Christmas game, with a thread, a shilling, and a wineglass, to answer questions, tell a lady's age, and so on. Astrology seems to have gained greatly increased attention, and in 1926 a popular paper published horoscopes for the days, and it was asserted at a Burnley inquest that the body of a drowned man had been found through the instructions of an astrologer. Corpses of the drowned have also been searched for repeatedly, and in a number of different counties during recent years, and even by the police, by the ancient means of floating on the stream or pond a loaf loaded with mercury. The loaf is expected to stay or loiter above the hiding-place of the body, but usually fails to do so. The observant reader will see certain divinations in constant use around him, especially by women, such as the never-failing "This year, next year, some time, never," in counting fruit-stones, buttons, etc.

Almost anything, approached in the right spirit, can be employed as a means of divination, probably with an equal chance of success. A delightful example was told in 1924 by an Oxford professor who had searched vainly for weeks for a library of cuneiform tablets. "In despair, and grasping a chance of divination, I went alone to the top of the mound, and chose a brick of the age of Nebuchadnezzar, which lay at my feet, and marked on it an arrow. Then, after blindfolding myself, and turning round many times to lose my bearings, I threw the brick backwards over my head. The next morning digging was recommenced at the place indicated by the arrow, and within two hours a large nest of valuable literary tablets was found."

ENGLISH FOLKLORE

The decrees of Fate may be discovered by active measures of divination to force their disclosure, or by passive observation of the shadows cast as omens of coming events. So many omens have already been mentioned incidentally in previous chapters that they may be dismissed very briefly now. The prevalence of fear of the future is shown by the overwhelming number of "ominous" presages, chiefly of death. Almost anything unusual- a falling picture, a cat dying in the house, rats nibbling the furniture, a broken mirror, a mole approaching the house, the howling of a dog, a cock crowing before midnight, the screeching of an owl, the breaking of the Christmas pudding, the stopping of King Henry VIII.'s astronomical clock at Hampton Court (occurred in 1924), a diamond crease from bad crossing of a tablecloth at the laundry, a horse whinnying at a funeral and a hundred other things- all betoken death. News is foretold by a moth settling on one or bees buzzing about the room, and a strange visitor by forgetting to put the lid on the teapot when making tea; but the list of omens might stretch on to the crack o' doom!

A whole chapter would be necessary for a list of omens from one's own body- spots on the nails for gifts, meeting eyebrows for those to be hanged or drowned, hair cast into the fire burning brightly for long life, tingling of the ears for scandal talked about one, itching of the nose for a coming vexation, itching of the right hand before receiving money and of the left before paying it, itching of the sole of the foot before treading on fresh ground, and even for our sneezes-

> "Sneeze on Monday, sneeze for danger,
> Sneeze on Tuesday, kiss a stranger, .
> Sneeze on Wednesday, get a letter.
> Sneeze on Thursday, something better.
> Sneeze on Friday, sneeze for sorrow,
> Saturday, see your true love tomorrow."

Even when we are dead the corpse continues to give its

omens, as if it does not stiffen there will be another death in the family within three months, and if the eyes do not close it is looking for a companion. Those who have staked anything on a risk find comfort in all sorts of omens. In 1926 I was told by one who had drawn Coronach in a "sweep" that he knew that this horse would win the Derby, as it did, because his wife saw two piebald horses on the preceding Monday. Dreams, in all their inconsequences, are much relied upon, but they go by contraries- e.g., to dream of a funeral three times makes matrimony certain- and tradition is followed in their interpretation rather than the numerous dream-books.

Days and seasons are still much regarded. In Worcestershire the wind will persist till Christmas in the same quarter as it is in at midnight on St. Clement's Day, and a bad fruit season in the Eyesham Valley is expected if the cuckoo is heard before Tenbury Fair (April 20) or after Pershore Fair (June 26). St. Swithin's Day keeps its repute for forecasting the weather for forty days, despite its annual discrediting. Great importance is attached to the flowing of intermittent streams after heavy rains- such as the three in Kent, the Drelingore Nailbourne between Folkestone and Dover, the Lyminge stream, and the Petham stream, the Lavants in Hampshire, and, before all, the Woe Water near Croydon. The latter is alleged, by Aubrey in the seventeenth century, as by many to-day, always to flow before a great national event. No notice is taken of the years in which its flowing has not been followed by anything remarkable, but a list is made of all chance coincidences with such occurrences as the Great Plague. It flowed in 1925, 1927, and 1928.

Besides the divinations deliberately made, and the omens which offer themselves, to forecast the future, there are many things which can be done or not done, or which may happen, and which will affect one's "luck." The folk do not usually regard life as a matter of mere chance, but rather as a matter of luck and, in part, of Fate. A woman, waiting for the arrival at a London cemetery of a funeral recently, was heard to say: "She was christened in church, and she was married in church, and now she's being buried in church! It's Fate!" Most people believe in luck, because it seems to explain many of the surprises in life, the accidents that seem to alter the whole course of a career, and the successes and failures that seem alike undeserved. It is not to be wondered at, therefore, that there is a long list of things to be done or not to be done, and others to be avoided or welcomed, for the sake of this luck, which almost seems a deity to be propitiated. In many cases the central idea is obvious of a whole group of beliefs hailing from different districts. For example, that it is unlucky to do anything out of its proper season seems to be why you must not eat an apple before St. Swithin's Day, bring into the house mistletoe or eat mince pies before Christmas, bring snowdrops in before the first chickens are hatched, and have a "palm" in the house before Palm Sunday, and why an engaged couple must not be godparents or be photographed together. A similar idea of ill-luck in impropriety seems to attach to two people passing on the stairs (which will lead to a quarrel), pouring from one teapot, or washing in the same water.

"Luck" dictates what must be done in many matters. You must not walk under a ladder, nor sit thirteen at table. In sweeping a room, you must begin by sweeping towards the center. As for cutting nails, most people know the rhyme beginning- "Cut them on Monday, you cut them for wealth," and ending "Cut them on Sunday, you cut them for evil, P'or the rest of the week you'll be ruled by the Devil!" It affects the household breakages also, for the charwoman or maid, after a first breakage, will resign herself to two more, and even select the most suitable articles. The same notion of triplicity applies to lighting three cigarettes from one match, and black once worn for mourning is expected to be worn three times. Sex taboos seem to survive in the ill-luck of meeting a woman on the way to work in the mines or in a fishing-boat.

In Northumberland she is specially unlucky if fair-haired

and flat-footed. To meet a chimneysweep is lucky, and in Leicester means a "good pay-day." Good luck is attached to everything deformed and crooked- a hunchback, crooked sixpence, etc. In London a bed must not be put across the boards, evidently a recollection that it was once held that death would be uneasy if the bed were across the beams or boards. Unlucky days, once very numerous in our calendar, are now represented by Friday (on which beds must not be turned nor many other things begun or done) and Holy Innocents' Day, still more unlucky. In Devon blankets must not be washed in May, or you will "wash relations away."

One of the most general beliefs is that it is unlucky to receive a knife or scissors as a gift without paying for it. In 1927, when Queen Mary was given golden scissors at Edinburgh to cut a ribbon, she is said to have insisted on paying sixpence for them, as "otherwise it would be most unlucky," and a similar payment is told of the Lord Mayor of London in 1928 at Felixstowe. The lucks of numbers (believed by many distinguished people, and including the extraordinarily lively objections to thirteen) and of colors cannot be dwelt on. "If you wear green you will soon after wear mourning." Hens are always set with an uneven number of eggs, or the eggs will be addled or the chickens will not thrive. For some lucks it is very difficult to suggest any explanation. Why, if (in Devonshire) anyone steps on the place where a donkey has been rolling, should evil soon follow? (I know that, in Devon also, a cure for whooping cough is to roll on the "form" from which a sheep must be turned off while dew is still on the field.) Why, before the war, should the playing of a German band be said everywhere to bring rain? Why should it be unlucky to keep your own hair combings?

Many very familiar lucky and unlucky things have not been mentioned- touching wood, unlucky houses and objects, etc.- but we ought not to pass over the "chains of luck" which for a number of years, right up to 1928, have worried nervous women.

You are requested to send a copy of the message to nine people, and then comes the threat of "luck," "Whoever does this will have great joy and happiness, but to those who neglect this will come misfortune. Do not break the chain. It was started on a Flanders battlefield."

CHARMS AND CURES, AND WITCHCRAFT, BLACK AND WHITE

In a certain Northern mining district, lots are drawn on "cavilling day," once a quarter, for the best working places in the mines. As the chance result seriously affects the household income, the wives are naturally anxious to influence it, and a favorite charm is for them to stand cross-legged and at the same time put the family cat into the oven. This is a specimen of innumerable charms to influence future happenings or to ward off ill which can still be found in use, in full faith, though often furtively for fear of ridicule. Although, as I stated in the last chapter, the love divination common fifty years ago has been largely ousted by vulgar fortune-telling, there are still girls in London and in many country districts who buy "dragon's blood" (the resin from the *Calamus draco* and certain other trees, used chiefly in varnish-making) to throw into the fire to regain a false lover, or burn "tormentil root" (*potentilla tormentilla*) at midnight on a Friday for the same purpose. An incantation should be recited with the dragon's blood somewhat to the following effect:

"Tis not this blood I mean to burn,
But my love's heart I wish to turn.
May he no pleasure nor profit see
Until that he comes back to me."

At Nottingham Shire Hall in 1927 a sentence of imprisonment was avoided by the refund of £97 which had been paid for a love philtre (consisting of a mixture of boracic acid and baking powder) to be used to "cure" a husband of unfaithfulness which was only alleged by a fortuneteller. Many charms involve spitting. The coster spits on his first takings of the day, and in Devonshire it is very lucky, if you find a piece of coal, to spit on it and throw it over your right shoulder. But the magical qualities of saliva are outside our present range.

Charming, especially for serious ailments, is generally the work of the white witch (most often a man) or wise-woman, who in a town would probably be called a "herbalist." The Times of 1920 tells us that in the East End of London a charm for scalds is for the herbalist to blow three times on the blisters, repeating the words:

"Here come I to cure a burnt sore.
If the dead knew what the living endure,
The burnt sore would burn no more."

But there is also a great deal of family and private practice, for medical and other purposes. For toothache you should sit under an ash-tree and cut your toe-nails. The Crediton Chronicle reported in 1914 that, when a Dorset auctioneer was on his way to have a tooth drawn by a dentist, a farmer friend begged him not to go, but to put his arms round a young ash-tree, make a slit in the bark where his fingers met, and then pull out some hair from the back of his head and put it in the slit. The surviving charms for the common ailment of warts are very numerous indeed. A common idea in them seems to be to count the warts and symbolically link them to something else which will decay, or be lost, and so carry off the warts. For instance, a stick may have notches cut to the number of the warts and then be buried, a parcel of pebbles of the same number may be thrown away, the inside of a broad-bean pod or a stolen piece of beef may be rubbed on the warts and thrown away or buried, a pin may be run into each wart in turn and stuck into an ash-tree, and so on. If anyone picks up the stick before it is decayed, or the pebbles, etc., the warts will be transferred to them.

The charms for whooping cough are almost as numerous. A small piece of the child's hair will be put between two pieces of bread and butter and given to a dog, to whom the disease is transferred. Or a saucer of milk is given to a ferret to drink, and then snatched from it and given to the child, and the ferret killed; a more humane form of this charm is to cut hair from the child's noddle, chop it fine, put it in milk, and divide the milk between the child and a ferret. In another charm the child is given a drink of milk in which a live trout has been made to swim. But perhaps the most interesting of all is to "break the cough" by taking children from North London to the Viaduct, Archway Road (Highgate), "the highest point in London, to get the four winds." (It is stated that there was a similar practice at Chelsea, sixty years ago, to take the sufferers to "breathe the seven winds" in the middle span of Old Battersea Bridge.)

In place of charming by a formula or by a symbolic or magical act, the end desired may be attained, more particularly if it is protection or the warding off of some sickness or other evil, by carrying on the person, or putting in the place to be affected, an amulet. The amulet may be something supposedly powerful in itself or made so by magical art. Few people have any conception of the extent to which amulets are now worn. It is, perhaps, as great as it was a century or two ago, though the purpose may be a little more vague, being in many cases for luck in general rather than for anything specific. Undoubtedly, if there is faith in them, they give the confidence which helps to success, and so strengthen belief. An East End doctor has estimated that 40 percent, of the children at the schools which he attended wear some sort of amulet under their clothes- i.e., not as an ornament, but as a protection. It is very difficult, however, to get direct information from the wearers, or even an admission of their presence. A very common amulet is a string of special blue beads worn as a preventive of chest ailments, both in London and in the country, and never under any circumstances removed. My wife showed such a string to a charwoman and asked if she knew anything about it, to which the woman replied, "No," after the suspicious fashion of those who think that you are "getting at them" in some way. But later in the day she said, "My Gladys wears a string like that you showed me," and, when questioned further- "Do you ever take it off, say, when you wash her?"- replied, very promptly, "Oh no! Then she'd catch cold."

The frequency of the wearing of amulets is attested by the newspaper references to them in the contents of the pockets of those found drowned or murdered. I have notes of many. A girl bludgeoned near Hull in 1926 had a lucky penny with a hole in it in her handbag; the body of a man drowned in the Thames in 1923 had a black-cat amulet in the pocket; a woman rescued from the Avon at Bath in 1921, who refused her name, was identified by the two lucky beans in her purse; the victim of a terrible murder at Liverpool that excited the country in 1913 had hung around her neck a medal of the (Japanese) "three wise apes"; etc. The war undoubtedly caused a very great revival in the use of certain classes of amulets, officers carrying them as much as men and affecting such things as netsukes. The baby's caul, which, as a preventive of drowning, was costly to buy during the Napoleonic wars, and had slumped to almost no value at all as sailing vessels decreased, again became a treasured possession in the days of U-boats, and is still occasionally advertised for sale.

A great foe, and fear, of the outdoor laborer is rheumatism, and many things are carried for it. Fishermen in the North and London gasstokers have the T-bone from the cheek of a sheep's head. Many people carry potatoes (which by their drying up show that the "screws" have gone into the tuber instead of into the joints), wear a silver ring (which blackens as it absorbs the evil), or trust in a mole's foot, pebble, chestnut, bit of coal, leather-covered little tube of mercury, piece of brick, or innumerable other things. It would be tedious to attempt a list of the amulets of old standing still in use- the hare's foot for cramp, the birthstone and zodiac rings of which some jewelers' shops make a feature, the rare surviving witch balls, the epilepsy ring made without payment from a half-crown of sacrament money, the holed stones, and the rest. Much more astonishing than the revival of some ancient amulets, however, is the enormous outburst of new ones, and importations and adoptions of foreign amulets, under the less "superstitious" name of mascots. There is even a London manufacturer of talismans designed on astrological lines. The word "mascot," which covers luck-bringing persons as well as objects, is derived from a Provengal word, *mascotte*, popularized by Audran's comic opera La Mascotte, first performed at the end of 1880. At the height of the craze, about 1922-1925, the chosen mascots were put upon nearly everything feminine- handbags, handkerchiefs, scarves, umbrella handles, bathing caps, and hats, and even "undies" were marked with the mascot instead of the monogram.

The fashion affects both sexes, and mascots are poured as lucky gifts upon candidates at by-elections, flying men, and football and cricket teams. Few motor-cars are now without some one of the innumerable forms, either inside the back window or on the radiator cap. They have even been adapted to advertising, and at the Wembley Exhibition you were invited to "stroke the lucky cat" in china among one company's exhibits, and Wills's issued cards of "lucky charms" with their cigarettes. The Great Western Railway Company in 1922 took advantage of the craze and distributed to its staff 50,000 copies of a small metal "charm against accidents- 'Is it safe?'" and expected them to be carried. The panel of the Insurance Acts has dealt a shrewd blow, that may ultimately be fatal, to the pharmacopoeia of the folk, though probably "cinder tea" and a few other nursery specifics will linger long. Folk medicine, for the most part, did little harm with its simple remedies, although there were bad exceptions, as there are among "patent medicines." In an inquest at Leeds in 1927 the police surgeon reported that the deceased had died from a dose, taken as a remedy for diabetes, of pigs' claws boiled, powdered, and made into a kind of tea. At one recent period the popularity of "dog grease" as a cure for rheumatism led to the decoying and killing of dogs in Blackburn, and to a prosecution before the magistrates. Some remedies are of very ancient date. The mouse was a child's medicine in ancient Egypt, and, when roasted or fried, is now regarded in Peakland as a remedy for whooping cough, and, when boiled, in London as a remedy for a certain lack of control during the night. The onion is an especial favorite, both as an amulet and as a preventive for smallpox; it was hung up in houses in Sheffield during a slight epidemic in 1927, and in 1924 near London slices were put between the stockings and soles of children to ward off whooping cough. Many of the folk think that the natural gifts of the seventh son of a seventh son are far more valuable in medicine than the mere professional training of an ordinary doctor.

A whole library of books, pamphlets, and magazine articles is in existence about witchcraft, and most readers will have some acquaintance with the subject, and a natural horror of the cruelty with which poor old women were pursued in the witch hunts. It is now almost two centuries and a quarter since the last execution of witches, though an old woman died from being ducked as a witch at Longmarston in Northants as much later as 1752. Fortunately we have at present neither to summarize nor to supplement the extensive literature already produced, but to inquire briefly whether the belief in witchcraft, and its practice, are any part of the folklore of today. This is not a matter on which strangers are readily admitted to confidence, and witches are not mentioned plainly until they are dead and no longer dangerous, but there seems to be clear evidence that in almost all quarters of the land the belief is latent and comes to the surface on occasion. The fortune-teller often carries out practices that are not easily distinguishable from those of the witch, and the white witch and wise woman maintain themselves in evidence not only by dealing with the "overlooking" so often suspected to be the work of the black witch, but by side lines of children's diseases and as herbalists and consultants on matters which in the town fall to the beauty parlor. The wise men are far more numerous than the witches. A few examples must suffice.

In 1915 the St. Albans Diocesan Gazette gave an account of a reputed witch in Essex, recently dead, whose ghost was laid in the traditional manner. A lady told the exorciser that before her death a neighbor had called and found her feeding her niggets, "those creepy-crawly things that witches keep all over them." In November, 1922, the Kingston county justices had before them a quarrel between neighbors at Cobham. The complainant's daughter said that the defendant had tried to stop her wedding by accusing the betrothed couple of practicing witchcraft. In 1923, at the Yarmouth Police Court, in a case of trouble between two women, a woman gave evidence that ten shillings had been paid to a witch for a spell on her sister, and her brother had to pay a pound to have it taken off. In 1924 a smallholder was charged at the Petty Sessions at Cullompton, Devon, with scratching a woman's arm so that it bled profusely, and with threatening to shoot her; the defense was that the woman had "ill-wished" him and bewitched his pig. In 1926, at Glastonbury Police Court, an application was made by an almsman for a summons for witchcraft against another almsman, who was said to have bewitched the former and his clock. In 1926 it was reported that a woman in Norfolk, who found her husband was attracted by another woman, was given, by a friend whom she consulted, the Lord's Prayer written backward, which she had to fasten under her blouse and keep there for three days each week until the husband changed; after a fortnight he would not recognize the other woman. At Tipton in 1926 two men were bound over for threatening an old woman who lived in a van, against whom several witnesses appeared, to say that they were terrified when in her presence and believed her capable of putting a curse upon them. The men said that she had put a spell over the wife of one and the sister of the other, who had had to be removed to a lunatic asylum. In September, 1926, a man was charged at Newton Abbot Police Court with wife desertion, and replied that he objected to her "witchcraft business." She had charged him with laying something on the rug to make his son ill, and when he went to sit in his chair he found it ringed by salt- i.e., a precaution against witchcraft. She had put articles belonging to him near her photograph, so that she might work spells with him. Finally, in 1927 a gypsy was charged at the Cornwall Assizes at Bodmin with obtaining £ 500 over a period of some years from a St. Mawes gardener to remove the effect of "ill-wishing,"

East Anglia and the West Country, from which come the majority of the above cases, may be looked on as the main strongholds of the faith witchcraft.

ENGLISH FOLKLORE

CONCLUSION

It will be appreciated that it was impossible in the preceding chapters to cite the authorities for individual items. As the volume is limited to folklore known to be living in very recent years, the sources are, in general, not books, but newspaper paragraphs, and especially reports of legal proceedings; but many items come from oral information, and others have been checked thereby. It was also impossible in most cases, and probably unnecessary, to define the exact area in which a particular practice is to be found, but it will be understood that few customs are universal over the whole of England, or are known to everybody in their particular area. Probably every reader who is interested in old beliefs and customs could add considerably to what has been written. It is to be hoped that he will make some note of his recollections, with date and place, for our folklore of the past lies chiefly in the memories of old people, and much of it will be lost as they slip out of the ranks. The items of folklore are no less precious, but much more perishable, than the fragments of pottery on which the archaeologist bases so much of his story. While several smaller nations, such as Finland and Estonia, have made remarkably full collections of their folklore, from which the national history can be enriched, England loiters behind, and it is to be feared that very much of the past has already been lost irrecoverably. A great amount of collection of facts is still necessary before the brilliant theories of the world within and without us, set out in more ambitious volumes, can be said to be broad based or more than hopeful guesses.

In Chapter III there has been an intentional omission to discuss a number of matters which it would have been difficult to deal with in few words, such as borough English, gavelkind, and many illuminative manorial customs. There has also been no mention of some large sections of the subject, which the exigencies of space shut out from other than the following very brief references:

Folktales: The roll of English traditional stories is a beggarly one, if compared with that of other nations, both those within and those without the British Isles. It is to be feared that few more ears can now be gleaned of what might have been the golden sheaves, for there is no reason to suppose that in early days our forefathers were less fond of a story or less imaginative than other peoples. Some of our tales have been kept alive, and spoiled, by guide-books. Probably a few short stories, and especially humorous stories or drolls, could still be gathered by the diligent, before "the wireless" fills every winter evening by the fireside.

Folk-Songs: Here our store is at least as rich as that of any others, and since 1898 the Folk-Song Society and Mr. Cecil Sharp have rescued large numbers from oblivion. As regards one section- "work songs"- by which is meant songs with rhythm and tunes adapted to aid co-operative work such as hay-turning, no extensive collection has been made, apart from seamen's shanties.

Folk-Music: Its peculiar characteristics and beauty are now appreciated, and much has been done to collect it since Chappell's National English Airs and Popular Music of the Olden Times appeared from 1838 onward.

Folk-Dance: This has come into great public notice since the foundation of the English Folk-Dance Society in 1911. Traditional dances still survive in a few bright spots. The Furry, or Flora, dance through the streets of Helston (Cornwall) on May 8 is well known by annual photographs. Another famous dance, the Abbot's Bromley Horn Dance, had fallen into disuse, but was revived in 1908.

Folk-Drama: Versions, however fragmentary, of any folk play or dramatic performance, and especially the mumming play, are urgently wanted before they vanish entirely, which seems likely to be with the generation now passing.

Proverbs and Sayings: Of these large numbers have been collected, but many are still current and have not been printed. If they appear to be a part of some story, like the saying "As throng as Throp's wife," it should be ascertained, if possible, what the story is. Many proverbs are the "moral" of forgotten stories.

Rhymes: Nursery rhymes, counting-out rhymes for games, and especially taunting sayings between villages, should be amassed. Here is one from the West Riding, which has not, so far as I know, been printed, and which expresses very well the local conditions fifty years ago, when I first heard it:

"Bradford for cash,
Halifax for dash,
Wakefield for pride and poverty;
Huddersfield for show,
Sheffield what's low,
Leeds for dirt and vulgarity."

Riddles: I do not think that there has been any systematic collection of riddles, nor are they likely to be as numerous as with some Continental nations, but the number already collected, as it were by accident, shows that there are probably more to come. Here, also, prompt collection is necessary. Here is a specimen from Oxfordshire:

"Long legs, short thighs,
Little head, and no eyes."
(Answer: A pair of tongs.)

Games: Lady Gomme's two valuable volumes (see Bibliography) contain descriptions, music, and songs of a very large number, and other collectors have dealt with smaller groups- e.g., string games- but there is yet a good deal of work to be done, as an American collector proved not long ago by his gatherings in the streets of London.

Folk-Arts: The only museum where these can be studied at present is, I believe, that at Haslemere, and the student has here a wide and almost unoccupied field, from which much can be learned about the racial spirit. Trade and local costumes, such as that still surviving among the "bondagers" or girl-workers of North Northumberland, should be noted.

To conclude, it may be repeated that the matters passed in review are by no means the whole, or even all the most important, of the current items of English folklore. Without its historical background of earlier beliefs the mosaic picture is much less intelligible, and even with it many pieces of the mosaic are still missing. Readers can, if they will, help to supply them.

BIBLIOGRAPHY

S. O. Addy: *Church and Manor.* (George Allen and Co.)

J. Brand: *Observations on the Popular Antiquities of Great Britain.* (Chatto and Windus.)

R. Chambers: *The Book of Days.* (W. and R. Chambers.)

M. Roalfe Cox: *An Introduction to Folklore.* (D. Nutt.)

Sir J. G. Frazer: *Folk-lore in the Old Testament; The Golden Bough.* (Macmillan and Co.)

Lady Gomme: *Dictionary of British Folklore, Part I.: Traditional Games.* (D. Nutt.)

Sir G. L. Gomme: *Folk-lore Relics of Early Village Life; Primitive Folk-Moots.* (Sampson Low and Co.) *The Village Community.* (Walter Scott).

S. Hartland: *The Science of Fairy Tales.* (Methuen and Co.)

W. Hone: *Every-day Book; Table Book; Year Book.* (Thomas Tegg.)

Eleanor Hull: *Folklore of the British Isles.* (Methuen and Co.)

Andrew Lang: *Custom and Myth; Myth, Ritual, and Religion.* (Longmans and Co.)

Publications of the Folklore Society. (Wm. Glaisher.)

ENGLISH FOLKLORE

C.J. Sharp: *English Folk-Songs*. (Novello and Co.)

R. J. E. Tiddy: *The Mummers' Play.* (Clarendon Press.)

E. Westermarck: *The History of Human Marriage.* (Macmillan and Co.)

THE END